Lectionary Tales
For The Pulpit

Series II
Cycle A

Timothy J. Smith

CSS Publishing Company, Inc., Lima, Ohio

LECTIONARY TALES FOR THE PULPIT, SERIES II, CYCLE A

Copyright © 1998 by
CSS Publishing Company, Inc.
Lima, Ohio

All rights reserved. No part of this publication may be reproduced in any manner whatsoever without the prior permission of the publisher, except in the case of brief quotations embodied in critical articles and reviews. Inquiries should be addressed to: Permissions, CSS Publishing Company, Inc., P.O. Box 4503, Lima, Ohio 45802-4503.

Scripture quotations are from the *New Revised Standard Version of the Bible*, copyright 1989 by the Division of Christian Education of the National Council of the Churches of Christ in the USA. Used by permission.

Library of Congress Cataloging-in-Publication Data

Smith, Timothy J., 1957-
   Lectionary tales for the pulpit. Series II, Cycle A / Timothy J. Smith.
     p.   cm.
   ISBN 0-7880-1217-7 (alk. paper)
   1. Homiletical illustrations. 2. Storytelling—Religious aspects—Christianity. I. Title.
BV4225.2.S55   1998
251'.08—dc21   98-9783
                                                                                                           CIP

This book is available in the following formats, listed by ISBN:
    0-7880-1217-7   Book
    0-7880-1218-5   IBM
    0-7880-1219-3   Mac
    0-7880-1220-7   Sermon Prep

PRINTED IN U.S.A.

Dedicated to

Donna, my loving wife

Rebecca and Matthew, my children

all of whom are a constant source of inspiration.

Table Of Contents

Introduction	11
Advent 1 — Matthew 24:36-44 Danielle's Laughter	13
Advent 2 — Matthew 3:1-12 The Exit Ramp	15
Advent 3 — Matthew 11:2-11 Jane's Encounter	17
Advent 4 — Isaiah 7:10-16 Mary's Christmas Letter	19
Christmas Eve/Day — Luke 2:1-20 Vicki's First Christmas	21
Christmas 1 — Matthew 2:13-23 Christmas Dreams	23
New Year's Day — Ecclesiastes 3:1-13 Love At The Library	25
Epiphany — Matthew 2:1-12 Vacation Of A Lifetime	27
Baptism Of The Lord — Matthew 3:13-17 Jack's Surprise	29
Epiphany 2 — 1 Corinthians 1:1-9 Day On	31

Epiphany 3 — 1 Corinthians 1:10-18 The Memorable Meeting	33
Epiphany 4 — 1 Corinthians 1:18-31 Send In The Clowns	35
Epiphany 5 — Matthew 5:13-20 TALK The Walk	37
Epiphany 6 — Matthew 5:21-37 Reconciled	39
Transfiguration — Matthew 17:1-9 Kevin's Vision	41
Ash Wednesday — Matthew 6:1-6, 16-21 Forest's Mark	43
Lent 1 — Matthew 4:1-11 Stealing Candy	45
Lent 2 — John 3:1-17 Larry's Boat	47
Lent 3 — John 4:5-42 Set Free	49
Lent 4 — John 9:1-41 I Left My Heart In Philadelphia	51
Lent 5 — Ezekiel 37:1-14 Henry's New Life	54
Passion/Palm Sunday — Philippians 2:5-11 Herman's Stand	56
Good Friday — John 18:1—19:42 Trek Of The Cross	58

Easter — Matthew 28:1-10 Home Movies	60
Easter 2 — John 20:19-31 Harry's Legacy	62
Easter 3 — Luke 24:13-35 Life From Death — Rick's Discovery	64
Easter 4 — Acts 2:42-47 The Joy Of Bible Study	66
Easter 5 — 1 Peter 2:2-10 Bruce's Integrity	68
Easter 6/Mother's Day — John 14:15-21 If Only I Had Known!	70
Easter 7 — John 17:1-11 The Cookout	72
Pentecost — Acts 2:1-21 A Gift Is Only A Gift When It Is Shared	74
Trinity Sunday — Matthew 28:16-20 What No One Told Karen	76
Proper 5 — Matthew 9:9-13, 18-26 One Bodacious Party	78
Proper 6 — Genesis 18:1-15 The Visit	81
Proper 7 — Matthew 10:24-39 Noelle's Summer Vacation	83
Proper 8 — Matthew 10:40-42 God's Direction	85

Proper 9 — Matthew 11:16-19, 25-30 87
 Ida's Attic

Proper 10 — Matthew 13:1-9, 18-23 89
 Seventh Grade Sunday School Class

Proper 11 — Matthew 13:24-30, 36-43 91
 And Then There Was Eve

Proper 12 — Romans 8:26-39 93
 Alice's Hindsight

Proper 13 — Matthew 14:13-21 95
 Aunt Betty's Advice

Proper 14 — Matthew 14:22-33 97
 Roller Coaster Ride

Proper 15 — Matthew 15:21-28 99
 Carla's Persistence

Proper 16 — Romans 12:1-8 101
 Rally Day

Proper 17 — Exodus 3:1-15 103
 Janice And The Bulldozer

Proper 18 — Romans 13:8-14 105
 The Defining Mark

Proper 19 — Romans 14:1-12 107
 Amber's Stand

Proper 20 — Matthew 20:1-16 109
 Ed's Vacation

Proper 21 — Matthew 21:23-32 111
 Two Brothers

Proper 22 — Matthew 21:33-46 Missed Out	113
Proper 23 — Matthew 22:1-14 Not At My Church!	115
Proper 24 — Matthew 22:15-22 The Word From God	117
Proper 25 — Deuteronomy 34:1-12 Broken Promises	119
Proper 26 — Matthew 23:1-12 Julie's Love Shines Through	121
Proper 27 — Matthew 25:1-13 Angie's Grand Adventure	123
Proper 28 — Matthew 25:14-30 Because We Care	125
Christ The King - Matthew 25:31-46 Take Me Out To The Ball Game!	127

Introduction

A colleague in a neighboring church was in the midst of a yearlong confirmation class. In the session which talked about worship he asked the seventh and eighth graders what they liked best about the worship service. While it is not unusual for young teens to find just about everything "boring," he was surprised that many of them answered, "The sermon." To be honest, he did not expect this. He pressed further, asking, "What do you like about the sermon?" Almost in unison they replied, "The stories." By the way, what these teenagers liked least was the singing.

Stories have a life all of their own. Good stories grab us and draw us into them. From my own experience I have discovered the power of stories in my sermons. When I am deep into some great biblical or theological truth I see the heads nod off, the eyes close. But as soon as I start a story people seem to perk up. They listen and they remember.

Good stories spark our own stories. Countless times persons leaving church will comment on one of the stories and occasionally tell me a similar story from their own life experience. The church I currently pastor is in the heart of Pennsylvania Dutch country. On most Sundays we have visitors from other places. I have been amazed how my stories seem to touch people I do not know and in all likelihood will probably never see again.

One particular Sunday stands out; it was one of those weeks when I struggled to find a good story to conclude my sermon. I had spent too much time searching for a good closing story. Finally, in desperation I found one in a ten-year-old magazine. On Monday evening I received a telephone call at the parsonage from a woman who had been in worship the day before. She was calling from her home in a neighboring state. It seems my concluding story touched her and her husband. She said they spent all day Sunday and all the way driving home discussing the story. She admitted that she had been struggling with a personal problem for a long time. The story had not only touched her, but for the first time she saw a solution to her dilemma. She said she believed there was a reason why she had worshiped in our church — as if God had led her there for a reason. She apologized for "bothering me" and asked me to mail her a copy of the sermon.

Through and with stories we can say things and be heard in a way that goes beyond simple prose. Equally amazing to me are the friends and members of the church who sometimes weeks and even months later will say, "You remember that story you told about ..." and then describe the story and how it touched them or made a difference in their thinking and on more than one occasion in the way they live their lives.

I am grateful for the opportunity to stand in the pulpit week after week to proclaim the good news of Jesus Christ. I am also thankful for the people that God has brought into my life. In this book I have attempted to tell stories based on real people and events. I hope that they might inspire a story from your own experience and empower your preaching in a fresh way.

Timothy J. Smith
September 1997

Advent 1
Matthew 24:36-44

Danielle's Laughter

"Keep awake therefore, for you do not know on what day your Lord is coming." (v. 42)

Five-year-old Danielle, along with her younger sister and brother, arrived in time for Sunday School on the first Sunday in Advent. As she looked around she knew something was different. Later, as Danielle and her family entered the sanctuary, she noticed all the decorations. There were candles surrounded by holly on the windowsills. There was a strange-looking wreath with purple candles on the altar. There was a Christmas tree covered with white Styrofoam crosses of all shapes and sizes over in an often-forgotten corner of the church. This was all new to her. She did not understand what all this meant.

In the moments before worship began Danielle asked her mother about the candles and the tree. Every five-year-old knows the colors of Christmas are red and green. Why were there purple candles? What were those things hanging on the tree? she asked. Her mother tried to explain as best she could, promising to tell her once they were home.

This proved to be no ordinary Sunday; something unexpected was about to happen. Obviously the adults were not in tune in the same way that Danielle was. She was filled with anticipation. She had difficulty waiting quietly in her seat.

The time came for the children's message. All the children made their way to the front of the church. The pastor had a habit of asking the children questions which more than one parent objected to — afraid of being embarrassed. "Good morning, boys and girls," the pastor began. "Who can tell me what today is?" he asked. One boy replied that it was Sunday; an older child came up with the right answer, "Advent." Danielle sat there smiling, taking in the conversation.

Then the pastor asked, "How do you know if you are awake or asleep?" At this moment Danielle burst into uncontrollable laughter. The sound of her laughter filled the sanctuary, traveling through the sound system. Her laughter was contagious. Soon some in the choir began laughing as well as persons throughout the sanctuary. The laughter energized the congregation in a way nothing else could. The pastor should have ended the service right then; there was no point trying to go on.

Yes, this was no ordinary Sunday, this first Sunday in Advent. Who better to remind us than a five-year-old?

Advent 2
Matthew 3:1-12

The Exit Ramp

"I baptize you with water for repentance, but one who is more powerful than I is coming after me." (v. 11)

He stood there at the exit ramp, an imposing figure. There was something about him that drew you to him while at the same time you were repelled by his appearance. His clothes were well-worn and dirty; he wore an old hunting cap; his hair was unkempt. He was unshaved. He looked as though he had not bathed in quite sometime — he was dirty. He had that glazed-over, spaced-out look on his face; either he was on drugs or completely stressed. He held a sign, sloppily written on a piece of discarded cardboard: "Will work for food." He stood there on that gray December morning at the end of the exit ramp as cars exited the highway. He did not move; he just stood there as cars lined up waiting for the light to turn green.

Chuck saw him standing there. He tried not to look at this man but could not help himself. He knew he did not want to make eye contact. If the strange man would look up Chuck would be sure to turn his head. There were several cars ahead of Chuck whose drivers seemed preoccupied, not paying any attention to him either. It was mid-December, after all, and people were busy and did not have either the time or inclination to help this poor soul.

As soon as the light turned, several cars whizzed passed him without even looking at him, without giving him even a second thought. Chuck was relieved when the light turned. Nothing was worse than seeing someone like that on your way to work, he thought. Chuck did not get too far down the road when his conscience got the better of him. Chuck had grown up in the church; he vaguely remembered something about helping those less fortunate. He recalled the time his youth group collected food and then went to a homeless shelter. But that was long ago. Now he had a job with responsibilities and a family besides. He knew he should have stopped; he could have stopped at a convenience store a half mile down the road and bought this man something to eat. It would only have taken a few minutes. Chuck tried to put this man out of his mind but he could not. It was as though his image was burned in his mind, like a photograph.

He had no more than pulled into his office complex when he turned around, heading back in the direction he had just traveled. This time he would stop and offer assistance. This time he would see to it that this man had something to eat.

Barely fifteen minutes later, when he passed that same intersection, the man was gone without a trace. He was not on the other side of the road. Even the cardboard sign was gone. All day long Chuck wondered what had happened to this unfortunate man.

He told his friends at work. One of his friends told him that his church was not only collecting food and clothing but was organizing teams to help find places for homeless people to stay. Chuck went to church with his friend the next Sunday; he told of his experience in the Sunday School class. "We have to do something," he told the class, offering to help out in any way possible.

His first inclination was right, that man standing at the exit ramp did have a message for him, a message from God.

Advent 3
Matthew 11:2-11

Jane's Encounter

"Go and tell John what you hear and see...." (v. 4)

Even though Jane's children were all grown and had families of their own, she still enjoyed attending the annual Christmas program each December. There were children from the nursery class who sang a Christmas carol. The first and second grade class came dressed as Mary, Joseph, shepherds, and angels. The third and fourth grade class performed an original skit about the true meaning of Christmas. The senior high students presented a contemporary version of the Christmas story that she particularly enjoyed. Jane said she comes to the Christmas program every year to help put her in the Christmas spirit.

Refreshments were served following the program in the Fellowship Hall. She watched as each child received a box of candy while parents and the other adults talked, ate a cookie, or drank punch. Jane scanned the room for someone who was not involved in conversation or busy with a child to talk with. She spotted Chuck. She was captivated the week before by Chuck's vivid description of the homeless man at the exit ramp. She did not have the opportunity to talk with Chuck other than just to say hello. Jane had something she wanted to tell him.

A couple of days after she heard him tell of his experience she had one of her own. She had spent the afternoon shopping for Christmas gifts for her grandchildren when she saw a homeless person standing in the middle of a divided highway, right outside of the mini mall. "I drove past him," she explained, "and then I thought of last week's Sunday School class. So I turned around, found a couple of dollars in my wallet and gave it to him." Chuck was touched that someone would be affected by his words the week before.

Jane's desire to help those less fortunate was rekindled when she had heard Chuck speak with such passion. They spoke for several minutes in the Fellowship Hall about what could be done not just at Christmas but all year long to help those with nowhere to stay or not enough food. Chuck said he was sure others at work would want to be involved, along with their Sunday School class.

Advent 4
Isaiah 7:10-16

Mary's Christmas Letter

"Therefore the Lord himself will give you a sign...." (v. 14)

Mary was a loving, thoughtful woman who took the time to write personal notes with her Christmas cards. She wrote in such a way that one could almost hear her voice. For five long years Mary had taken care of her bedridden husband. As her husband's illness progressed he was unable to communicate or do anything for himself. He just lay there. Several times each day she would lovingly feed him, talking to him. Mary continued to care for him even though some friends suggested she find a nursing home. The few minutes a visiting nurse stopped to check on her husband several times a week were the only time Mary was able to leave her house to run errands. It was understandable why Mary was always in such a hurry and out of breath. Mary never seemed to mind, making the most of her few minutes. The letter told how her husband had died on Christmas Day evening the previous year.

Mary's Christmas letter was positive and full of good news that would lift anyone's spirits. She told of going on vacation with her daughter's family to California. She had a wonderful time, visiting the sights of Southern California. She told of spending the night on the Queen Elizabeth in Long Beach and being in the audience for the taping of one of her favorite game shows. Even though she was not picked as a contestant, she wrote, she could be seen as the camera panned the audience. One could not help but think, "Good for you." Mary was finally able to do what she had been unable to do for so long. Finally she was able to enjoy herself.

Her Christmas letter went on to detail her involvement at a local shelter for women and children. Two nights each week Mary volunteers her time to help in any way she can; these women and children are going through difficult times. Mary has a wonderful way with children. She told how she would play games with them at the shelter. At other times she just listens as the women tell their stories of abuse and broken relationships. Mary offers words of hope and encouragement. "Things will get better, dear," she says, patting a hand.

Again Mary's friends thought, "Good for you." Mary continues to show Christ-like love to those who most need that love in their lives. Mary is indeed a special woman. Her Christmas letter was an inspiration.

Christmas Eve/Day
Luke 2:1-20

Vicki's First Christmas

"The shepherds returned, glorifying and praising God for all they had heard and seen, as it had been told them." (v. 20)

Life was anything but easy for Vicki. She had experienced more than her share of problems, being raised in a home where she never experienced love. She herself was a recovering alcoholic and drug addict. Her life had been hard. She looked a lot older than her 27 years. Through her struggles Vicki and her husband tried their best to raise their two young children.

They did not have much to call their own — as far as earthly possessions. They lived in a small apartment which was furnished with old, discarded furniture. The sofa was covered with an old blanket to hide the burn holes. Nothing could hide the smell.

Vicki's journey to wholeness was assisted by her landlady, Ruth. Ruth did all she could to help Vicki and her family. She told them not to worry when their rent was several days late. "Pay me when you can," this kind older woman told them. One day Ruth told Vicki that she should attend church. She explained that her children would not only enjoy Sunday School but would benefit from it. Ruth was a Sunday School teacher and told Vicki that her children could go with her each week, which they did for several months.

Before too long Vicki started attending worship. It was a new experience for her. She was filled with questions each week which kept the pastor on his toes. It was obvious that Vicki wanted to learn. She never had the opportunity to attend Sunday School as a child. She desperately wanted to put her old life behind her. Ruth would talk with her during the week and Vicki would call the pastor with her questions.

As the Christmas season approached the children were given parts in the annual Sunday School Christmas program. Her daughter was an angel, dressed in a white sheet with a gold pipe cleaner halo carefully hovering above her head. Her son was a shepherd, who stood with the other shepherds in the background with Mary, Joseph, and the Baby Jesus in the forefront. The night of the program Vicki brought her husband to church for the first time. The program went off without a hitch. Mary and Joseph entered on cue, as did the shepherds and angels.

The next week was Christmas Eve. Vicki wanted more than anything to attend. She sat almost spellbound as the choir sang beautifully. In candlelight the pastor read the Christmas story from Luke's gospel. The sermon was about God's love's for all people which came down to earth at Christmas. The service concluded with an invitation to go to the altar to pray. Before the pastor even finished Vicki was kneeling at the altar. There were tears streaming down her cheeks; her eyes were aglow. Something wonderful had happened to her that night. She experienced for the first time God's unconditional love. It was during the service that she realized the depth of God's love for her and everyone.

A week later she attempted to describe as best she could what had happened to her. "I never really understood Christmas before," she said. "It was always just a day, a holiday, a day to get gifts." Now she said she understood the real meaning of Christmas. Even the Christmas carols she loved to sing since she was a little girl took on new meaning.

God loves the world so much that God sent Jesus to be our Lord and Savior.

Christmas 1
Matthew 2:13-23

Christmas Dreams

"Get up, take the child and his mother, and flee to Egypt...." (v. 13)

Jeff and Cheryl had a dream. Actually they had the same dream. They dreamed of traveling to a distant land to get a child. Cheryl looked at Jeff with utter disbelief as they ate breakfast. "I had the exact same dream," she told her husband. Jeff wondered what all this meant. They had talked about adopting a child from another country but never followed through. Now that they both had the same dream, they were convinced that this was what God wanted them to do. They wanted more than anything to make a difference in some young child's life. They had the means to improve one child's life and that was what they wanted. This was what God wanted them to do; the dream confirmed it.

They began gathering information about adopting a child from another country. There were children living in terrible conditions that they wanted to help. After several months a six-year-old girl was found half-way across the world in the former Soviet Union. "That's our girl!" Jeff announced to Cheryl. They began learning how to speak Russian.

Their travel plans included a flight to Moscow, where they would be picked up at the airport by another couple. All the arrangements were in order. If they had any doubts, it was about the health condition of the little girl they were about to travel half-way around the world to pick up. It was explained to Cheryl and Jeff that often the health of a child was exaggerated so the government officials would allow the child to leave the country. It would be harder to adopt a child if the child were in perfect health, they were told.

It was just like their dream as they boarded the plane. After an exhausting flight they arrived. They were met and taken to an apartment. Their only trouble so far was with communication, since they knew very little Russian and their host knew even less English.

The next day they met the young girl they would adopt as their daughter. She smiled at them. She had spent some time living in an orphanage but seemed eager to be a part of a family. They were told that her father had been killed and her mother was seriously ill in a hospital.

The following afternoon they boarded another plane bound for the United States. Their new daughter seemed pleasant and bright, yet on that long flight they had trouble communicating with her. Jeff said, "I had to tell her a hundred times in Russian, 'Don't do that' as she continued to kick the seat in front of her."

Jeff and Cheryl took the young girl to their home and welcomed her as part of their family. She responded with love and affection. What this girl needed most was love, and Jeff and Cheryl could provide her with that.

New Year's Day
Ecclesiastes 3:1-13

Love At The Library

"For everything there is a season, and a time for every matter under heaven." (v. 1)

On New Year's Day Jay had an opportunity to reflect on his life's journey. Although he had experienced some bumps along the way he was thankful for the people God had brought into his life. When he hit his lowest point God had just the right people there to help him through.

He had hit bottom just three years before. He bought a gun from a hardware store and planned to end his pathetic life. He placed the gun in his mouth and pulled the trigger. Nothing happened. He went back to the store to return the defective gun, telling the clerk the gun was defective. Then he bought some rope and tried to hang himself from a tree but the branch snapped, hitting him on the head. Nothing ever seemed to go his way.

A couple of days later, still filled with thoughts of suicide, he spent the last of his money for a bus ticket. "I just wanted to get away," he explains. "I wanted to go as far away as my $18 would take me." It would be easier to commit suicide elsewhere, he thought. When he arrived in the city he was in such bad shape that a security guard would not let him leave the bus terminal. The security guard personally took him to a shelter. Jay would spend the next six months living at that shelter. During the day he would roam the streets, eating his meals at several church soup kitchens in town.

As winter approached he sought cover indoors and found the public library. Other homeless people spent the day in the library to escape the cold. Sandra, one of the librarians, spotted Jay and offered to help him. "If it wasn't for the librarian," Jay claims, "God knows where I'd be right now." The librarian was a kind

Christian woman who took the time and energy to help him. She suggested several books that would help him. Jay had nothing else to do so he began reading the books Sandra gave him. Included were books on living the Christian life. That winter Jay read more books than he had since he was in school.

Sandra would spend her lunch hour talking with Jay. She told him that Christ could help him. Jay was open and receptive to this woman's love for him. Love had been the missing ingredient for most of his life. Knowing that someone cared about him, that someone loved him, was what helped Jay turn his life around. Jay acquired a new perspective on life, thanks to Sandra, who even helped him find a job. He began attending Sandra's church where he found other caring and supportive people who offered to help him.

Jay worked hard, continuing to read his Bible and attending church. Soon he found an apartment in the same neighborhood as the shelter. Others would complain about the bad neighborhood, but not Jay. He would share his positive outlook with others. He wanted to stay close so that when he wasn't working he could help others. The Mission coordinator speaks highly of Jay: "He's encouraged others to go the way he went."

On New Year's Day he prayed, giving thanks to God for the people who helped him to turn his life around. He knows there are areas he still needs to improve but takes each day as it comes. Of his new life, Jay explains, "I don't have any problems, really. I keep life simple."

Epiphany Sunday
Matthew 2:1-12

Vacation Of A Lifetime

"They set out ... ahead of them, went the star that they had seen at its rising." (v. 9)

Phil and Paula, along with their four young children, planned a two-week vacation in the western states. Their plan was to fly to Denver and then rent a car and drive through the Rocky Mountains. As their vacation date approached the entire family was excited. This would be their first visit out west. They would have two full weeks to enjoy the sights without worrying about the hassles of their jobs. It would be wonderful.

When they arrived in Denver they were so happy. The older children stood taking pictures of the distant mountains while the young children took pictures of just about everything else. They had made plans but did not want to be on a tight schedule so they could enjoy themselves.

Something unexpected happened on Saturday afternoon. As they were driving on a deserted section of the highway they hit a deer. Fortunately no one was hurt but the rental car could no longer be driven. By this time they were close to five hundred miles from where they rented the car. They were stranded for several hours in the middle of nowhere, Paula explains. When help finally arrived it was late in the afternoon, so they checked into a motel in the nearby town. Paula called the toll free number of the car rental agency to inform them what had happened, hoping they would be able to get another car the next day so they could continue their vacation. Nothing like this had ever happened to them and they hoped the car rental company would be able to help them.

The next morning, Sunday morning, Phil told Paula that he and the children were going to church. When they were home they attended church every week. Faith played an important role for this family. Paula said she would stay in the motel room and try again to call the insurance company and the car rental agency. She did not know what they would do if they could not get help.

Phil and the kids discovered something at the church they had not anticipated. People from the church cared about them even though they had never met them before. Phil explained what had happened and how they were stranded without a car. The people in that church showed love and concern for them. One family invited them to Sunday dinner. Another family offered them the use of their fully equipped van for the day. The man handed Phil the keys. He said there was a state park sixty miles away that would be great for them to visit. "You go and enjoy yourself," he said smiling.

Paula could hardly believe it. She had spent an hour with no luck trying to get help from the car rental company, which left her frustrated. Meanwhile her husband and children went to church only to discover people who cared about them. They were total strangers and they were offered the use of a van. Paula wondered how they knew they would return with the van. This was a lesson in faith and trust that Phil and Paula would not forget. God was with them on their journey.

Baptism Of The Lord
Matthew 3:13-17

Jack's Surprise

"...just as he came up from the water, suddenly the heavens were opened to him and he saw the Spirit of God descending like a dove and alighting on him." (v. 16)

Jack was one of those people that when you first met him you immediately liked him. There was no pretension in what Jack said. He told it like it was in his kind and gentle way. At the monthly men's fellowship breakfast Jack wasn't afraid to talk of spiritual matters, often catching others off guard. When conversation centered on the trivial Jack would turn the conversation around, discussing more important matters of life and faith. It was obvious that he took his faith seriously. He spoke openly and honestly of his own life and his estrangement from God. He told how he was able to make peace with God. There was a note of urgency in Jack's voice. Jack was on a different timetable than all the other men. Jack had been fighting cancer for five years and knew he would not be able to keep fighting it. At first the doctors gave him six months. "But I showed them," he said with a smile. "I'm still here." He enjoyed the monthly breakfasts, stating several times he wished they would meet more often.

Jack asked to speak with the pastor for a few minutes following one of the breakfasts. He had been thinking of joining the church for a while, with the encouragement of his wife and mother-in-law. Now he was ready to join. "There's one thing I want you to do for me," he said before he left. "Don't tell my wife or mother-in-law. I want to keep this a secret." He laughed, saying, "I can't wait to see the look on their faces." A date was set for Jack to join the church the next month. The pastor promised not to tell anyone.

At the next men's breakfast Jack said he wanted to share something with the group. He told them that he would be joining the church in a couple of weeks. He had put off joining for too long. Now he was ready. This caught several of the men by surprise. One said, "I thought you already were a member, you've been coming for so long." "No," Jack replied, "I never got around to joining." He thanked the men for their positive influence in his life and helping him make this decision. Jack wanted to share this with the group, knowing that they would want to be present. He also made them promise not to tell anyone. "I don't want Jane or Ruth to find out," he said.

The day arrived when Jack would join the church. When he was called forward he purposely walked to the back of the church to get his mother-in-law. This was his moment, the moment he had been waiting for. With his wife on one arm and his mother-in-law on the other he proudly walked up the center aisle. At the altar of the church, where he had knelt several weeks before, he now professed his faith and took his membership vows. Everyone knew Jack was so happy. You could see it in his big smile. His friends were also happy. Although no one would admit it, some were a little choked up.

Jack touched many lives during his courageous five-and-a-half-year battle with cancer. Just three short months after joining the church Jack died with his wife, Jane, and mother-in-law, Ruth, at his bedside. Men at the monthly breakfast fellowship continue to speak with affection and admiration for their friend, Jack.

Epiphany 2
1 Corinthians 1:1-9

Day On

"God is faithful; by him you were called into the fellowship of his Son, Jesus Christ our Lord." (v. 9)

Early in January the students in Ms. Clark's ninth grade social studies class were learning about Martin Luther King, Jr. They watched a video tape of Dr. King's life, which included his famous "I have a dream" speech. Ms. Clark asked the class what they could do to honor Dr. King on their day off from school. She explained that we best honor someone when we do something that person would do. There was silence at first, revealing that perhaps the students had never thought of doing anything out of the ordinary. It was an uncomfortable silence, with coughs, clearing of throats, and the shuffling of feet under the desks. "Come on," Ms. Clark challenged, "what can you do in honor of Martin Luther King?" Just then the bell rang. "I want you to come back tomorrow with some ideas," the teacher said as the students hurried out of the classroom.

After school Aaron and Ted were talking about this assignment. To be honest they hoped to sleep in and then hang out or play video games on their day off from school. They wanted to do what they usually did on days off from school. Ted said he remembered hearing something at his church about fixing up some older homes in the city. "Could you find out?" Aaron asked. Ted promised he would check it out and get back to him before class.

The next day Ms. Clark asked her students about what they could do for other people. Several students suggested that they could help homeless persons at the various shelters in the city. Another said she could help her mother around the house. Aaron and Ted proudly told the class that they were going to fix up a house in the city. "Sounds like some wonderful ideas," Ms. Clark told the class.

At the early hour of 8:00 a.m. on their only day off of school all month Aaron and Ted, along with others from the church and community, reported for work. The boys spent the entire morning in the basement of an old rowhouse shoveling sand, water, cement, and lime into a vat. Their project was to shore up the crumbling foundation wall. It was hard work in less than perfect working conditions. These two young men felt the satisfaction that they were doing something to help another person. They took pride in what they were doing. "It's better than going to the mall," Ted would later tell his class.

When they finished in the early afternoon Aaron looked down the block at the other houses. "This is only one house," he said. "This is only one day. There are a whole bunch of dilapidated houses just falling apart. This should be an ongoing thing." This was just a start; there would be other days, and they could ask their friends and neighbors to help out with this project.

Ted explained the next day in class, "I kind of wanted to give something to the community, to see what I could do." Ms. Clark was pleased with their effort. She told them Dr. King would also be pleased with their efforts.

Epiphany 3
1 Corinthians 1:10-18

The Memorable Meeting

"Now I appeal to you ... that all of you be in agreement and that there be no division among you, but that you be united in the same mind and the same purpose." (v. 10)

The church meeting erupted in contention over, of all things, a new piano. Some at that meeting were absolutely convinced that the church could not survive another Sunday without a new piano. Others were equally persuaded that the present one, which they pointed out several times was bought as a memorial, worked just fine. "I called my friend," one of the women informed the group, "who has worked on pianos all his life. I asked him, could a piano ever wear out? He told me he did not think so. It probably just needs a tune-up or something." Those on her side nodded in agreement while those desperately desiring a new one got angrier.

A choir member stood up and said, "The piano we have right now was not made to be played in church." "It worked just fine all these years," someone shouted in opposition. Back and forth the two sides went for what seemed like an eternity. As the meeting dragged on there was an edge in people's voices. Tempers were flaring. It was obvious that just about everyone was irritated with the whole situation. Before anyone realized it the meeting had turned ugly.

It was at this turning point that Frances stood up. She had not said a word throughout the entire debate. Frances was an older woman who never said a negative word about anyone, which was why she was loved and respected in the church. "I've heard just about enough of this," Frances said as she might break up a fight between her grandchildren. "I hate to see this happening here at our church. We are the church! We need to set an example for others," she said. "No one will want to come to our church if our members are fighting like this."

There was silence. Her words hit home like a ton of bricks. After a few minutes of awkward silence Ralph, the chairperson, thanked Frances for her words. The unity of the church was important. "If all we do is fight," he reiterated, "no one will come." No one knew what to say, so after several more minutes of silence Ralph asked the pastor to dismiss the meeting with a prayer, seeking God's guidance in this manner. A date was set for another meeting the following week. Before people left for home there were clear signs of reconciliation as persons shook hands and some even hugged. Everyone realized that things had gotten out of hand. They had Frances to thank for her courage in reminding them that they were the church.

During the next several days persons on both sides of the disagreement phoned Frances to thank her for her words of wisdom. "I always have the best interest of the church in mind," she replied. The next week at the meeting a compromise of sorts was reached in a spirit of love. Actually it was Frances' idea that everyone quickly adopted. It was agreed that a new piano would be bought and that everyone on the committee would sell frozen pizzas and sandwiches at their jobs and around the community to raise money. The fund raiser would last several months before enough money would be raised to purchase a new piano.

Epiphany 4
1 Corinthians 1:18-31

Send In The Clowns

"God chose what is foolish in the world to shame the wise...." (v. 27a)

It certainly was a risky thing to do — to invite clowns to participate in the worship service. This particular congregation did not engage in foolishness. The people sat there in the pews always looking serious, never smiling. After all, church was supposed to be serious, at least that was what they were taught. The previous pastor began sermons with humorous stories which the people unmercifully complained about. Many a conversation centered around the inappropriateness of telling such stories in church.

If the congregation had known that morning as they went to church that clowns would be leading worship that day, they might have stayed home and watched Charles Stanley on television.

As the worship service began two clowns entered the sanctuary, one on each side. They were dressed in clashing colors, baggy pants, orange and red hair and, of course, a bright red rubber nose. The clowns were handing out colorful balloons as they made their way up the aisle. To say that the congregation was surprised would be an understatement.

Once up front the clowns performed a couple of skits which were meant to loosen up the congregation. In a subtle way the clowns were poking fun at the seriousness of the congregation. One of the short skits was about loving one's neighbor. In it the two clowns engaged in a mock battle over a property line, pushing and shoving each other. The lengths these clowns took pointed to the folly of such disputes. By this point some of the congregation were smiling while it was obvious that others were quite annoyed.

Following several more short skits one of the clowns removed his red and orange wig and rubber nose. In earnestness the clown described his clowning ministry. He would visit area hospitals and nursing homes. "You would not believe some of the patients that are in the hospital," the clown said. "Some have given up on life, yet," he explained with obvious delight, "when they see us, something wonderful happens to them, smiles return to their faces." Some were moved to tears as he told of an encounter in the children's ward. One of the mothers told him it was the first time her daughter had smiled and laughed since before her illness. The laughter had a positive healing effect on the patients. The week before the clown was in a nursing home and was asked to visit a resident who never had any visitors. When he entered her room it was dark, the drapes were drawn, the lights were off. She just lay in bed, not wanting to communicate with anyone. He admits that it took much effort to reach this woman, but he kept trying until she smiled and later spoke with him.

"You look at me and see a clown," he told the congregation, "but when people who are hurting or lonely look at me they see the face of Christ."

After church someone was heard commenting, "You know those clowns really had a good message to share after all."

Epiphany 5
Matthew 5:13-20

TALK The Walk

"No one after lighting a lamp puts it under the bushel basket, but on the lamp stand, and it gives light to all in the house." (v. 15)

A group of mothers has been meeting once a month to pray for their children, as well as for other students and the teachers of the local elementary school. Their concern stemmed from what their children would be exposed to once they started school. The mothers prayed that God would show them a way to instill positive character traits in the children. For a couple of years the moms discussed ideas that did not pan out. The school district was not supportive of the idea of pulling students from their classes for one hour of Christian instruction a week. Some of the mothers were also uncomfortable with that notion. So the moms continued to pray and wait.

The opportunity presented itself when the school district initiated a character education program. Two of the moms in the prayer group were asked to join the committee. "It was the answer to our prayers," one of the mothers said. "I truly think it was God's timing." An after-school program was designed, Tuesday Afternoons Live for Kids, known as TALK, with the full support of the school district. The program would meet at area churches and would be open to students in third through sixth grade. The moms' excitement was contagious; others soon joined in support. Other moms soon volunteered to help along with several retired school teachers who would help the students with their homework. Area pastors would also be involved, taking turns presenting a character trait each week. Additional time would be designated for activities, crafts, and snacks. After several months of planning they were ready to begin the program.

The question remaining was would the students want to take part in this program? Brochures were sent home the first week of school. Their goal, as stated in their mission statement, was "to promote positive character development and personal growth by using stories, songs, games, activities, Bible memory work, and peer discussion." At the annual open house at school several TALK representatives were present to answer any questions and enroll the students.

"The response was unbelievable," the volunteer director reported, "with over eighty students signing up that night." There were so many students that some had to be placed on a waiting list.

It took a lot of work to pull resources and people together but it was well worth it that first day when eighty students entered the church. For many it would be the first time they had been inside a church. Tuesday afternoons became a time of learning and fun together. God had answered the prayers of the moms' group.

Epiphany 6
Matthew 5:21-37

Reconciled

"... leave your gift there before the altar and go; first be reconciled ... and then come and offer your gift." (v. 24)

No one could remember when the trouble between Mark and Sue began. Their differences of opinion had caused a major rift between them at work.

Mark was new to the job, eagerly looking forward to a fresh start with a new company in a new city. Sue, on the other hand, had worked for the company for a decade and knew the other workers well, as well as the intricate workings of the company. In Mark's mind it seemed as though Sue and her friends were ganging up on him. It seemed that they were forever trying their best to make Mark look bad in front of the other workers and the boss. Mark confided to a new friend, "They are not even giving me a chance to prove I can do the job."

Before too long Mark and Sue stopped speaking altogether. Mark would walk past Sue without looking at her — without speaking to her, not even a "hi" or "hello." Nothing. Even though Sue stopped speaking with Mark she felt secure in her position. After all, she had been with the company for many years. It wasn't as though she would be the person to lose her job. The conflict bothered Mark a lot more than Sue because his job was on the line as well as his reputation.

Before too long it became obvious to the other employees that Mark and Sue were not able to work out their differences. They were not as productive as they should have been either. Mark will admit that after a certain point he stopped trying altogether. A consultant, Hank, was brought in to try to patch things up. Hank invited both Mark and Sue into the conference room hoping that they would be able to work out their differences. First Mark was given the opportunity to share his perceptions of the problems he was having with Sue. "She has been trying to sabotage my work since my first day on the job!" he bemoaned. "That's not true," Sue said defensively. "I guess I was just joking around." Hank's skill was in bringing people with problems together. He interjected that maybe Sue felt threatened by Mark. Not only was Mark younger, he had just graduated from college with a specialized degree, something Sue did not have. Both Mark and Sue pondered that statement.

The next step was to bring Mark and Sue to speaking terms. Hank explained that it was important for them to look at each other when they spoke. When Mark told his side he looked at the floor or at Hank, or at a painting on the wall, at anything but Sue. When Sue spoke she looked at Hank, avoiding so much as even eye contact with Mark. "It is important to look at each other when you speak," Hank told them. Reluctantly Mark looked at Sue and continued. Sue looked up at Mark. The conference ended with a small breakthrough. The first important step had been taken toward reconciliation. They agreed to try to work together, not to allow their personal differences to interfere with their work.

Still Mark kept his distance, not going out of his way to avoid Sue, but nonetheless trying to avoid Sue as much as possible. Sue, on the other hand, was making an honest attempt to be friendly and to speak with Mark every chance she had. This went on for several weeks until Mark recognized Sue's effort and also began making some effort to restore their broken relationship.

Eventually Mark and Sue became friends and they remain friends. Once they were able to understand each other better as well as themselves, they were able to start over in their relationship and soon discovered that they actually had common interests.

Transfiguration Sunday
Matthew 17:1-9

Kevin's Vision

When the disciples heard this, they fell to the ground and were overcome by fear. (v. 6)

Kevin often daydreamed about mountain climbing, not just any mountain, but Mount Washington in upstate New Hampshire. Wouldn't it be great, he would think to himself, to scale the mountain. All the hikers he spoke with had their own story or knew stories about the famed mountain. There was the intrigue of climbing the highest mountain peak in the northeastern United States. Then there was the challenge of climbing a mountain knowing that many people never made it to the top.

One day Kevin decided he would attempt to climb the mountain. He began planning for his trek two months before he would embark. This was all he talked about. His friends and co-workers were probably tired of hearing about Mount Washington every day. As part of his preparation he read all he could about Mount Washington, the history as well as the legend. He bought the necessary provisions he would need for such a trip, including a tent and plenty of dried foods to take along with him.

No one really knew how much Kevin was looking forward to his trip as he counted down the days before he would leave. He planned to spend ten full days climbing and camping. Kevin was experiencing some personal problems, just little things that seemed to pull him down. There were some problems with the people he worked with. They accused him of taking all the overtime for himself. "He only ever thinks of himself, never considering other people's needs," one of his co-workers told the boss. He was also having some problems in his relationships as well. He had not spoken to his parents for several months. It seemed every time he talked with them it would turn into a shouting match. Kevin claimed that his parents still treated him as a child and not as an adult. Kevin recently broke up with his long-time girlfriend. She told him in no uncertain terms that she never wanted to see him again. No one knew how much Kevin was looking forward to getting away from all his problems. Ten days of peace and quiet. Ten days away from his critical co-workers, his parents, and his former girlfriend. Up on the mountain he could forget his problems.

The warm sun felt good on Kevin's face as he began his hike up the mountain. Even the air that he breathed refreshed him that first day. It took Kevin a couple of days to reach the summit. He was in no hurry, above all he wanted to take his time and enjoy himself. He had found those days of solitude peaceful. As Kevin would later tell a friend he had "time to think." During those days Kevin thought of many things. He fondly remembered his childhood camping trips with the Boy Scouts, his high school friends he had lost track of, his hope of getting married and starting a family. He found the climb both tiring and invigorating at the same time. It was a good feeling. For the first time in a long time Kevin felt alive as he went higher and higher up the mountain.

Kevin had a big smile on his face when he reached the summit. He had made it, he had accomplished what others could not. It was a proud moment. He found a place and sat down. He spent an hour just looking out over the majestic beauty of the mountain. From his vantage point he could see tourists traveling up the mountain in vans. He watched the people and felt good about his achievement.

In that beautiful setting Kevin realized that his problems were not permanent but with some effort they would pass. In the majesty of the moment he experienced the presence of God in a way he never had before. Kevin stayed on the summit for a full day before he started back down. When Kevin left for home he had a new focus and much needed new perspective on life.

Ash Wednesday
Matthew 6:1-6, 16-21

Forest's Mark

"But when you give alms, do not let your left hand know what your right hand is doing...." (v. 3)

Forest never said much when he came to church. He would sit in the last pew on the left with his brother-in-law every week. In all his years he seldom missed a Sunday. Persons meeting Forest for the first time would immediately notice his big smile. He was always upbeat and cheerful, never seeming to have a bad day. He dressed well, wearing a coat and tie each week to church. He had retired ten years before after working in the family car business his whole life. Young people who did not know him well would view him as a nice, quiet older gentleman who came to church each week, but that was all he did.

Early one summer Forest was scheduled for routine surgery and later diagnosed with cancer. By the end of summer he died.

After his death the truth about Forest came out. It was then that people throughout the community as well as the surrounding area began talking about Forest. There was one gentleman who said he had bought cars from Forest for many years. "Every car I ever bought I bought from him," he said. There was something about Forest that made people trust him. He had a way about him that made people feel comfortable around him. An elderly woman told how when her car needed service, he would drive to her home to get the car and then bring it back later that afternoon. Another person told how he did not have enough money for the repairs and Forest allowed him to pay his bill when he could.

There was one family that was experiencing financial problems, and mysteriously there would be a bag of groceries on their porch each Friday. There was never a card or note or anything to identify who had brought the food each week. The family did not know where the food came from until several weeks later when one of the children spotted Forest's blue Chevy pulling out of the driveway.

Forest would always take the time to talk with people, which was one of the reasons he was so loved. No one seemed to know all the good things he did in his community. Forest was a man who helped people on a regular basis without letting anyone know. He never took credit or wanted public recognition for what he did, he just did what his faith required of him without fanfare. This was how he lived out his faith.

Lent 1
Matthew 4:1-11

Stealing Candy

"... All these I will give you, if you will fall down and worship me." (v. 9)

Mark was one of those teens that other kids wanted to be with; at the same time parents strongly encouraged their children to stay clear of him. Being told to stay away from someone had the opposite effect. The neighborhood kids were drawn to him like a magnet. Whatever Mark was doing, whether playing ball or just walking around, others would soon join him. Was it his attitude or his cockiness? Parents knew just by looking at him and talking with him that he was trouble. Mark was the youngest of three children. He was in his early teens when his family moved into the neighborhood from another part of the state. Mark was quite popular at school and in the neighborhood. Some would sneak out with Mark. One mother went to school late one summer to have her son's class changed so he would not be influenced by Mark.

Teenagers hate to admit it when their parents are right, but in Mark's case they were. One day at the convenience store Mark stole a piece of candy. No one saw him take it, not even the other boys who were with him. As the boys were walking home Mark pulled candy out of his pocket, much to the shock and amazement of the others. "It was easy," Mark bragged. "It was only candy," Mark explained nonchalantly. "It's not as though they are going to go broke over a couple of pieces of candy." The other boys swore that they would not tell their parents what Mark did. The only purpose it would serve would be that they would not be allowed to do anything with Mark. They made a pact not to tell anyone. It would be their little secret.

The next week the boys again walked to the convenience store. This time the boys kept a close watch on Mark. If Mark was going to steal something they would see him. The boys were intrigued with the whole notion of taking something and getting away with it. Stealing from a store went against everything that their parents and Sunday School teachers taught them. They were always taught that stealing was wrong and people who steal would be arrested and placed in jail. They watched as Mark again stole some candy when the clerk turned. Unfortunately a couple of the boys stole some candy along with Mark. As soon as the boys were outside Mark proudly announced, "See how easy it was. She doesn't even know I took anything!"

If Mark got away with stealing something, then others could too, especially with Mark's encouragement. The temptation was too great for several of the young people. Some of the others would eventually part company with Mark.

Lent 2
John 3:1-17

Larry's Boat

*"Very truly, I tell you, no one can enter the kingdom of
God without being born of water and Spirit." (v. 5)*

It wasn't as though Larry was a bad person — he certainly was not. He was a Christian, a loving husband, a caring father, a hard worker, a friend to many, and someone who would always help a neighbor in need. First impressions do not always reveal a person's true character. When persons first meet Larry they would mistakenly think he was angry at someone or something. He would strike people as someone who was angry at the world.

Larry did not feel comfortable attending church on a regular basis. The truth was he was infrequent at best, especially in nice weather. Some in the church tried to suggest or maybe rationalize that Larry had a disagreement with the pastor and that was the reason he wasn't in church. But that wasn't true. Deep down Larry just did not have any desire to attend church.

Instead Larry would travel an hour and a half to the bay where he owned a 25-foot sailboat. Larry loved his boat. It was there that he would spend his weekends from late spring through early fall each year. After working indoors all week Larry enjoyed feeling the sun beating on his face, the wind beneath his sails; he loved everything about the bay including the smell. Larry delighted in being independent, doing what he wanted to do when he wanted to do it. Larry's boat on the bay was the perfect solution to his wanting to be independent. Larry's weekend journeys continued for the better part of a decade. Periodically he would attend church — but you could tell his heart and mind were elsewhere.

Every once in a while Larry would feel a twinge which he attributed to God, but he was always able to dismiss it. He might go to church for several weeks at a time or volunteer to help paint

Sunday School classrooms to placate this notion. It was after Larry retired after forty years with the same company that spending weekends at the boat lost their appeal. Larry was ready for a new challenge, a new adventure, so he signed up for a Bible study at a neighboring church. It would be an intensive nine-month Bible study. Larry knew it would be hard work but felt it was something he had always put off, claiming never to have either the time or inclination.

No one would say that Larry did not take the Bible study seriously. Each week he always completed his assigned readings. He would ask insightful questions as well as make astute observations. As the study continued it was obvious that something was happening to Larry.

Near the end of the nine-month Bible study Larry described his experience. "It was like all the pieces of the puzzle fit." Over the years, he explained, he got bits and pieces of the Bible from his mother or Sunday School or through his own personal study and even occasionally through sermons. But now everything seemed to fit together into a whole. It was as though one important piece was always missing. Now through this Bible study everything fit together nicely for the first time in his life.

The next year Larry became the Sunday School superintendent. He wanted other people to experience what he did. He set a personal goal of starting a Bible study at his church within a year's time. Larry sought persons who might be interested; he would teach the class himself. His enthusiasm was contagious. Larry was a man of his word, and the next fall he embarked with eight persons in Bible study.

Lent 3
John 4:5-42

Set Free

"It is no longer because of what you said that we believe, for we have heard for ourselves, and we know that this is truly the Savior of the world." (v. 42)

Ken grew up thinking he was no good at anything. To say he had an inferiority complex would have been an understatement. Deep down he felt he could never do anything right. This attitude affected his entire outlook on life — the way he did everything. If you were to ask Ken's parents they would tell you that they were good parents. They never physically abused any of their children, never beat them, never locked them in the closet or anything like that. They had a nice new home in the suburbs, new cars, and the children had an ample amount of toys. Each child received a brand new bicycle one Christmas. To outsiders they seemed like the ideal family.

The problem arose in the way they treated their children. Specifically it was the words they used, their attitudes toward their children that robbed the children of positive self-esteem. "You're stupid" or "Can't you do anything right?" were often heard at the dinner table. When Ken was in his teen years his parents still treated him like a child, as if he couldn't do anything for himself. Ken would frequently overhear his mother say she didn't know what kind of a job he could ever get since he could not make change from a dollar.

In his twenties Ken still lived at home with his oppressive parents, afraid to step out on his own. His parents continued to discourage him from moving out. Whenever the subject came up, his not-so-loving parents would tell him he did not have enough money to live on his own. What would he do to wash his clothes, never mind the fact that he did not know how. How in the world could he even afford a washing machine? his mother asked him one day. Ken was convinced that if he ever moved out on his own he was bound to fall flat on his face.

Then one day in a fast food restaurant Ken met Lynn. Just joking around he asked Lynn if she would like to go out with him, expecting she would immediately say no. To his great astonishment she said yes and they began dating. An amazing thing happened to both Ken and Lynn. They both changed as a result of feeling loved for the first time in their lives. Friends commented on the change in Ken; he almost seemed like a different person. Ken and Lynn loved and affirmed each other. Two years after they met they were married.

After they were married for a while Lynn asked Ken if he would attend church with her. While growing up the church had played an important role in Lynn's life, while Ken rarely attended. At first Ken only went to church to please his wife. If going to church with her made her happy then he would go — after all, he told himself, it was only for an hour.

Something unexpected happened. While attending church Ken discovered the Living Christ for himself. He listened to the words about abundant life and soon claimed that life for himself. Once he met Christ he could not turn away. He wanted the abundant life that only Christ can offer and it changed his entire life.

Lent 4
John 9:1-41

I Left My Heart In Philadelphia

"Here is an astonishing thing! You do not know where he comes from, and yet he opened my eyes." (v. 30)

When Barbara and Charlie joined the church they spoke of it as being a homecoming. It was time for them to return and it felt good. As they were greeted by others they were smiling and obviously happy.

The next summer Barbara and Charlie were in church. The sermon that morning was from a member of the church, who spoke of breaking bad, destructive habits. The message struck a cord with Barbara, she could certainly identify with it. A couple of days later Barbara was rushed to the emergency room with an apparent heart attack. Neither of them knew how serious the situation was until the doctor spoke with Charlie. He was very matter of fact: the situation was very serious. He was just trying to keep her alive overnight and then in the morning she would be transported to a university hospital in Philadelphia. Barbara's heart was failing. If she was to live she would need a heart transplant.

"The hardest part for me," Barbara later explained, "was seeing terror in the eyes of my sweet Charlie and my three kids as the crash cart was rushed into the room along with at least eight doctors working on me." The next Sunday Barbara was fitted with an artificial heart pump which would keep her alive until a donor heart would be located. Barbara and Charlie were comforted by the fact that she could live on the pump for several months, but were told she probably would have to wait a couple of weeks until a suitable donor heart might be available. Charlie took a leave of absence from work so he could be by Barbara's bedside each day. Barbara's three adult children visited her in the hospital. It was the first time in years that her whole family was together in one place. Somehow this life and death struggle brought them closer as a family.

The days of waiting quickly turned to weeks. Barbara spoke of her love for her husband and her love for her church. People in the church sent her notes of encouragement as well as gifts to let her know she was in their prayers. Barbara responded by writing notes to the congregation which were read during Sunday morning worship. In her first letter she wrote, "Never take anything for granted." Her letters told of her experience, of waiting, of her love for Charlie, and of her faith in the God who loves her. She would end her letters with "I love you all. God bless you always." Her letters touched the congregation in an unexpected way; people looked forward to hearing additional letters the next week.

Through her ordeal of waiting for a donor heart Barbara was in good spirits with a positive outlook. Repeatedly she placed her faith in God, knowing that God would not desert her in her hour of need. The Heart Failure Unit was on the 21st floor of the hospital. Barbara and Charlie quickly made friends with other patients; some had better prognoses and others were in worse shape. She witnessed to her faith in Christ to other patients. She would walk through the unit, stopping in each room offering a word of hope. With her artificial heart pump beating inside of her, like the ticking of a clock, she was able to offer words of hope to people who seemed to be running out of hope. The summer wore on, Barbara and Charlie continued waiting. "Maybe this week," Barbara would say to those who called her.

On Labor Day evening Barbara and Charlie received word that a donor heart had been located. Less than an hour later she was wheeled to the operating room. There were complications in the operation. Barbara lost a lot of blood and received several transfusions. She was once again near death. The doctors were able to save her life through heroic actions. She received her new heart. When she awoke her husband was once again beside her. He encouraged her, "Honey, you are going to make it." Several days later, while in the hospital cafeteria, Charlie saw the doctor who had saved his wife's life. He greeted him with a hearty handshake.

"Thank you from the bottom of my heart," he told the doctor, "for saving my wife's life."

Barbara was weak from the operation and less than a week later caught a virus which would send her to the Critical Care Unit. Once again her life hung in the balance. She became so weak that she was unable to breathe on her own and was hooked up to a ventilator. She was given megadoses of anti-bodies to fight the infection. Recovery was painstakingly slow for her. She would remain in the Critical Care Unit for ten days.

A month later she was transferred to a rehabilitation hospital where she would have to learn how to walk again. Barbara was wheeled to the roof one unseasonably warm October afternoon. It was the first time she had been outside for over three months. Later she said, "You would not believe how good it felt to feel the sun on your face." That first day as she sat there the tears flowed. By mid-November Barbara was more than anxious to return home. She also looked forward to returning to church.

Doctors and friends cautioned her about being out in public too soon. She was still very susceptible to colds. But nothing could stop her determination to return to church. With her husband at her side, still having visible trouble walking, she made her way to church in December. She requested that the hymn "Amazing Grace" be sung because that was how she viewed her life and her second chance at life. Tears once again flowed from her eyes. It was an emotional moment in her life and in the life of the congregation.

Lent 5
Ezekiel 37:1-14

Henry's New Life

... Our bones are dried up, and our hope is lost; we are cut off completely. (v. 11)

Henry hit bottom. Perhaps what made the situation worse was that he knew he hit bottom. "Before the night was out," he stated matter of factly, "I knew I would either be in jail or dead."

Serious problems do not crop up overnight and neither did Henry's. As soon as Henry and Nancy were married they begin receiving applications for credit cards. In just a couple of months they had credit cards from every department store in the county as well as several national cards. It did not take them too long before they were in debt over their heads. "At the time," Henry explains, "Nancy was working part-time earning $150 a week and spending $300." The hole kept getting deeper and deeper, making it harder and harder to climb out.

Their financial problems soon led to marital problems. Henry and Nancy had known each other for five years before they got married. During their courtship they very seldom argued. Once they were married the arguing began. Their credit problems certainly did not help the situation.

One thing led to another, their financial problems led to problems in their relationship which led Henry to drink. When he finished working he did not want to go home, so he would stop off for a couple of drinks. At first he would be an hour late coming home. Nancy would be waiting for him with dinner. It made her mad when Henry came home late, especially when he never called her. As the weeks passed Henry came home later and later. There were nights when Henry did not come home until the bar closed at 2:00 a.m.

One day everything came to a head. The credit offices of the department stores began calling every day wanting an explanation of why they were late with their payments. Henry's boss did not actually say it — he didn't have to — if Henry's productivity did not soon improve he would have to look for someone else. Late that night when Henry finally made it home he found Nancy still awake. It was obvious that she had been crying as she waited for him. She told him if he didn't soon straighten out she would leave him. "She meant every word," Henry said.

After hearing that, Henry went back out to drive through he dark streets of their town. He was so upset he did not know what he would do. He needed to blow off steam but was unable to find any release for his anxiety. So he drove and drove through the quiet streets of one neighborhood after another. In his drunken state he soon became lost, which upset him all the more. He was cussing loudly out the window at no one but himself.

Henry is a little fuzzy about what happened next. He does not remember driving into a church parking lot. Somehow he managed to park and soon fell asleep. A couple of hours later he woke up and realized he was in a church parking lot. The only light was shining through a large stained glass window. He stared at the window for the longest time until he recognized that it was Jesus. Jesus with his arms stretched out as if wanting to embrace him. It was then, at that moment, that Henry realized that he needed to make some radical changes in his life. It was in that church parking lot that he realized he needed help.

Henry spent the rest of the night there, thinking about his life and praying to God that somehow he could turn his life around. He startled the church secretary and pastor as they arrived the next morning. He told the pastor what had happened to him, seeking help and guidance. They prayed together. Henry made some promises to God that morning: from that moment on he would be a Christian, he would be a better husband, a better worker, and a better person. He knew it might take a while for him to straighten out his life, but he was committed and confident to begin.

Passion/Palm Sunday
Philippians 2:5-11

Herman's Stand

Let the same mind be in you that was in Christ Jesus....
(v. 5)

Herman is a courageous Christian who is not afraid to take a stand even if others might perceive it as unpopular. He wanted to limit the number of liquor licenses in the township. "There are more places with liquor licenses than there are churches," he said, "three or four liquor establishments to every one church."

Herman prayed for guidance in this matter while at the same time doing research. He discovered that if he collected enough signatures the question of liquor licenses could be placed on the spring primary ballot. He made some telephone calls, trying to get others to help him in his effort. He was interviewed by the local newspaper. He explained his views on the subject, certain that the majority of the residents would agree with him to limit liquor licenses. He cited statistics about alcohol abuse as it related to accidents and domestic relations in the state. Herman arranged for several area churches to hold drive-through petition signings. He worked hard to get the word out. The day before the drive-through petition signing Herman was interviewed by the local television station. The next evening there was a report from one of the churches showing a driver signing the petition.

In the thirty days Herman had to collect signatures two things happened. First, he fell short of his goal of 25 percent of the registered voters. He had to admit that he did not have the support he thought he would. Second, he was unmercifully criticized. Much of the criticism was nasty and mean-spirited. There were letters to the editor of the local newspaper, claiming that Herman was "holier than thou" and judgmental. The day after the petition drive ended the local newspaper, on the front page in bold letters, proclaimed

"**Prohibitionist's Effort Fails.**" He received much mail at home that was critical of his stand. One restaurant owner wrote telling him how such action would severely harm the township because there would be enormous loss of income as businesses would locate elsewhere, which would translate into higher taxes for residents. Another restaurant owner told how he makes donations to community causes and how concerned he is in regards to the community, but he thought Herman's approach was all wrong. Even his answering machine often contained critical messages left by anonymous callers.

The spark was missing in Herman's eyes as he was portrayed in negative, critical ways. Through it all his friends saw a different side of him, a side they had never seen before — humility. "At least I tried," he said in an uncharacteristically soft voice. Herman accepted the criticism; he accepted defeat. Yet, regardless of the opinions of others, he believed that he had the best interest of the community in his heart.

Good Friday
John 18:1—19:42

Trek Of The Cross

So they took Jesus; and carrying the cross by himself, he went out.... (19:16b-17a)

It was easy to miss the small town nestled between the mountains. The last half century had not been kind to this community. Upon graduation an astonishing 65 percent of young people would move away to attend college or find employment. Most would never return to live in that community. As a result, the majority of the people in that town were senior citizens. Many of the homes were old, in need of serious repair. This community lived without hope, their best days were long past.

Each year on Good Friday the community would gather at 12 noon in front of the Methodist church for the annual Trek of the Cross. The Trek of the Cross would proceed down one street and up another, stopping off at each of the three churches in that small town. The idea of the Trek was Elmer's. He wanted to do something for the community, knowing that many persons were unable to attend church. Elmer would portray Christ as he had for the past ten years. Not only would he look like Christ, he would walk barefoot through the town. His nephews would play the part of Roman soldiers leading him through the streets. Others would join the procession; some would be wearing biblical garb while others would be dressed in regular clothing. As the Trek got more publicity people from nearby towns would come, some to join in the Trek, others to sit in lawn chairs along the sidewalk to watch. The next morning there would be a somber picture in the local newspaper of Elmer dressed like Christ, complete with a crown of thorns.

The Trek became a special moment for the people living in that community. Elmer's nephew explains, "You could tell instantly that they were reminded at that moment of what had happened."

Elmer portrayed Christ in such a way that persons were drawn to him although he would never draw attention to himself. For several years a young woman in a wheelchair would join in the Trek. Those experiencing personal problems would somehow feel revived after having walked through town with Christ. The Trek became Elmer's visible statement of faith.

On the final stretch before returning to church Elmer noticed Helen sitting on her porch. Helen was suffering from cancer and wasn't expected to live more than a couple of months. When Elmer spotted Helen he did something he had never done before in his ten years of portraying Christ in the annual event. He broke from the guards, walked up to the porch, and embraced Helen. Tears flowed down Helen's face as well as the faces of the others participating in the Trek. "That's what Jesus would have done," someone said later. It did not take long for everyone in the community to learn of this act of love. Everyone was talking about it. This was the real message for Good Friday.

Easter
Matthew 28:1-10

Home Movies

Suddenly Jesus met them and said, "Greetings!" And they came to him, took hold of his feet, and worshiped him. (v. 9)

One evening, for some unknown reason, Kay found herself alone in her basement watching old home movies. Kay's children were busy with outdoor activities so she went to the basement for some much-needed solitude. She was feeling rather melancholy without knowing why. As she watched the old flickering 8mm movies, which she had not seen in years, she immediately recognized her grandmother. It was wonderful to see her grandmother alive years after she had died, if only on the old home movies. Kay had not known her grandmother when she was young and healthy. In the movie her grandmother was the picture of health and vitality. She had died when Kay was not quite a teenager.

In the movie her grandmother was standing in front of their row home in the city. It was Easter Sunday as her grandmother, young mother, and aunts were getting ready to go to church. Her grandmother was wearing a beautiful blue dress with a flower pinned to it, while her mother and aunts proudly wore Easter bonnets. Kay remembered hearing her mother tell her that on nice days the family would walk to church. What struck Kay that evening was how her grandmother was smiling. She did not remember seeing her grandmother smile much. What she did recall was her grandmother's suffering with a lengthy illness. Kay could not help but be drawn to her grandmother's smile.

In her anxiety Kay said out loud for no one to hear but herself, "If only she knew what would happen to her." In the movie her grandmother seemed so healthy. If only life could return to that simpler time when families went to church together. The movie seemed to have a message for her, if only she could freeze frame that idyllic scene: the smiling face of her grandmother, who would not find out about the disease that would claim her life for another thirty or more years. Kay wondered if her grandmother would have been smiling had she known what would happen to her. Upon further reflection Kay realized that in the movie her grandmother was close to Kay's present age. Like her grandmother at her age, Kay did not know what the future held for her either. As Kay thought about these things she found tears in her eyes.

As she sat watching home movies Kay recalled her grandmother's funeral. She remembered the words of the pastor who told everyone present that they would one day be reunited with their loved ones. Those words seemed to calm her thoughts. Those long-forgotten words were reassuring for Kay as a young girl and now years later they gave her a sense of peace.

Her grandmother showed her something important, something she would never forget, and that was her faith in Jesus Christ. Even as her illness progressed she held firmly to her faith. Her grandmother lived and died with the assurance that God would take care of her and never desert her. Sitting alone in her basement Kay reconnected with her grandmother if just for an instant. She understood that she was with God. Kay's own faith was rekindled. Her grandmother left her something precious — something that she wanted to give to her children and, God willing, someday to her grandchildren.

Easter 2
John 20:19-31

Harry's Legacy

Thomas answered him, "My Lord and my God!" (v. 28)

Harry was a quiet, gentle, kind-hearted man who daily demonstrated his concern for people. He was a pastor for over forty years, serving his last church for twenty years. When it came to preaching Harry had a style all his own. He was not what might be labeled flashy; he certainly was no showman. Harry had the gift of making people feel at ease. Whenever anyone wanted to speak with him he always made that person feel welcome and comfortable. He always had time for his parishioners, and never gave the perception that he was too busy to speak with anyone who wanted to talk with him. The adults in the congregation looked to Harry as the kind father. For the children and youth Harry was the ideal grandparent. When he retired the congregation that he had served so well gave him and his wife a once-in-a-lifetime trip to the Holy Land.

It was not long after they returned from their trip that Harry got a part-time job as a grocery bagger at a local supermarket. Even though he was retired he still had energy and still wanted to be around people. Besides, he figured, they could use the extra income. A warm smile always greeted persons as they checked out. He would occasionally offer an encouraging word to someone who shared a problem or concern. His popularity was among the children. In addition to always speaking with the children in line with their parents, Harry would often have a hand puppet in his pocket which he would bring out and speak in a funny voice to the children. The children loved him and every time they went to the supermarket they looked for the kind old man. Whenever his puppet would appear there was always laugher. Harry was an ambassador of goodwill among the employees, who soon came to love him.

At first people from his former congregation felt uncomfortable seeing their retired pastor bagging groceries. Soon they would talk with him on their way out of the store. Before too long, like the children, adults would look for Harry every time they shopped. Harry always had an encouraging word, a word of hope, to offer people.

For 23 years after his retirement Harry bagged groceries. Then one winter Harry fell and broke his leg. He would no longer be able to work at the supermarket.

It was while Harry was home recuperating that a trusted colleague stopped to see him. With enthusiasm Harry told how he was studying his Bible. Currently he was once again reading the book of Romans. He showed his friend his Bible where he was making notes in the margins. His friend was surprised that Harry would find not only strength but fulfillment in reading his Bible, something he had done all his life. As his friend left he told Harry that he hoped he had as much desire to immerse himself in the word of God when he reached his age.

Easter 3
Luke 24:13-35

Life From Death — Rick's Discovery

Then their eyes were opened, and they recognized him; and he vanished from their sight. (v. 31)

Rick asked the pastor if he could say a few words to the congregation on Sunday. It would be his first time back to church following a several-month illness. Knowing Rick the way he did, the pastor said it would be all right for him to speak.

Rick was nervous on Sunday morning as he made his way to the pulpit. "I admit that church was never a high priority for me," he began. He explained that he had good intentions; it was just that other activities always seemed to crowd out the church. He told how he hadn't been feeling well for a couple of weeks before he went to the doctor. He endured a battery of tests before the doctor told him what he feared the most: cancer. Rick went home and cried. For the first time in his life he felt there was nothing he could do to remedy the situation. He asked that question most people ask in that situation, "Why me?"

It was then after hearing this devastating news, that Rick began attending church more regularly. It became a source of hope to him. He told the people in his Sunday School class about his illness. His name was added to the prayer list. He took comfort knowing that people at the church showed concern for him as he was about to undergo surgery followed by several weeks of chemotherapy.

The people of that church did more than just pray for him. Members of his Sunday School class visited him at the hospital. The day he went home from the hospital some women from the church helped clean the house. Another couple made arrangements for a hospital bed to be delivered and set up at his home. "Don't worry about how much it costs," they told him. "Concentrate on getting better." Others brought food to him, including homemade soup which was the only thing he could eat when he was so sick. When he was well enough people would talk to him on the phone, which he really appreciated. Others sent him cards and notes of encouragement. There was a gentleman from the church who did not deal well with illness but wanted to help, so he came and mowed the grass each week.

Rick was touched by the others' kindness. He felt like the Lord had come into his home to help him. To be honest, he said, he felt bad that he had been a member of the church for so many years without ever doing anything to help anyone else, and now here were all these people helping him.

He told the congregation that once he turned his illness over to the Lord he felt peace. Then his priorities changed, which altered his entire outlook on life. He wanted to say a few words to the congregation to thank them for their support during his illness and recovery. "I never would have made it," Rick told the congregation, with tears welling up in his eyes, "without you people in the church."

He valued the importance of life after his experience of deadly illness and now viewed each day for what it truly was — a gift from God. He thanked the pastor for giving him the opportunity to say a few words and then went back to his pew. This was one of those Sundays when the pastor really did not have to preach a sermon, Rick already had.

Easter 4
Acts 2:42-47

The Joy Of Bible Study

They devoted themselves to the apostles' teaching and fellowship ... And day by day the Lord added to their number those who were being saved. (vv. 42a, 47b)

Patty longed to study and gain a better understanding of the Bible. She had reached a point in her life when she realized she did not know much about the Bible. What triggered this desire was her teenage daughter asking questions for which she did not have any answers. Her daughter participated in a youth Bible study. She would come home and share insights that Patty knew nothing about. What frustrated her the most was that she could not answer her daughter's questions.

Patty tried a Bible study at her church but found it rather disappointing. It seemed to her that they spent too much time singing and on seemingly trivial matters and not enough time learning about the Bible. When she would ask questions the others would look at her almost in disbelief. No one had an answer for her either. They had their opinions but they could not find the answer in the Bible, which left Patty totally baffled. It did not take too long before Patty stopped attending Bible study; she told herself she could do better reading the Bible on her own. Patty shared with a friend at work her desire for more knowledge of the Bible. Her friend admitted a similar interest and together they went to her friend's church to participate in a Bible study. There really wasn't too much difference between that Bible study and the one at Patty's church; it was rather disappointing.

When the new pastor arrived, fresh from seminary, Patty made an appointment to see him. She explained her longing to be part of a real, honest-to-goodness Bible study. She explained how the Bible studies she had attended just did not meet her expectations.

She was at a point in her life when she wanted more than simple answers. The pastor listened carefully to what Patty told him. The pastor agreed to start a Bible study if Patty could find a half-dozen people to attend.

A month later Patty had talked several people into attending a new Bible study. Maybe it was the pastor's inexperience, but for that Bible study he used one of his seminary text books. Patty and the others each bought a copy and began reading it. Patty learned about the cultural background of various books and other facts which helped her understand the Bible in a new way. The more she read and studied, the more the scriptures came alive for her.

Patty says that was the best Bible study she had ever attended. That year she learned more about the Bible than at any other time in her life. The more she learned, the more she grew in her faith. As a result Patty became involved in the life of her church, doing things she had never dreamed of doing. The next year she would lead a beginners' Bible study. Now Patty and her daughter can have in-depth talks about the Bible.

Easter 5
1 Peter 2:2-10

Bruce's Integrity

But you are a chosen race, a royal priesthood, a holy nation, God's own people, in order that you may proclaim the mighty acts of him who called you out of darkness into his marvelous light. (v. 9)

No one was expecting the announcement that Bruce would retire after many years serving on the state legislature. He was loved by the citizens he represented, having won all his re-election bids easily. People could hardly believe the news that he would retire. It would certainly be difficult to find someone to fill his shoes. Bruce decided it was time to step aside to let someone else have the opportunity to serve his state. He was in office longer than anyone from that district. During that time he had served both the district and the state well. Bruce still had a year to complete his term and vowed to work harder than ever before.

As his term was nearing completion, he was invited to speak at various groups and clubs within the district. He was at the height of his popularity and found he could say things he might not normally say. As a guest at a monthly prayer breakfast, Bruce told the audience, "I profess Jesus Christ as my Lord and Savior!" It was refreshing to hear an elected official, a career politician, publicly profess his faith in Christ. There were several state officials, Bruce said, at the capital who would meet for breakfast and prayer on a regular basis. He was grateful for the opportunity to share with this group of dedicated Christians. As he went about his business in the state capital he felt supported and upheld by the prayers of his sisters and brothers.

Bruce shared an experience: he was running for a leadership position within the state government. Above all, he said, he wanted to run a clean campaign. He would not resort to mud-slinging or name-calling, which had become popular campaign techniques. He lost his bid for leadership but he said he felt good about the way he had campaigned. As Bruce spoke it was obvious that he was a man of values and integrity, guided by his faith in Christ.

He said he had wanted to win but since he did not, he accepted his fate. A surprising turn of events took place after his defeat. His colleagues gained a new respect for him. They saw a side of Bruce that they had previously not seen. As a result many new doors of opportunity were opened to him. It was ironic that in losing a coveted position he actually received more power and prestige than he would have had he won in the first place.

As a result of that experience, Bruce found that he was taken seriously and frequently asked his opinion in critical manners. Various groups would approach him asking if he would represent them. He would be retiring from public office, but he would still serve his community and state as he had all his adult life.

Bruce was firmly grounded in his faith and did not shy away from sharing it with others.

Easter 6/Mother's Day
John 14:15-21

If Only I Had Known!

"If you love me, you will keep my commandments." (v. 15)

Diane, by her own admission, was a difficult teenager who often gave her mother a tempestuous time. She described herself as being willful, stubborn, and independent. Frequently Diane would stay out well past her curfew, and several times she did not return home until the next morning. Notes were sent home from her teachers, informing her mother of her misbehavior at school. There was even that time when a police officer brought her home, having arrested her for underage drinking. By her actions Diane made life very trying for her mother. Through all Diane's rebellion her mother never gave up on her. She never stopped loving her. She never stopped hoping and praying that somehow her daughter would change. Her mother just gave and gave. She gave unselfishly, not receiving anything in return but grief, yet she constantly showered her daughter with love and affection. Her mother never gave up on her.

When Diane was old enough, she moved away from home, telling her mother in no uncertain terms that she would never return. For nearly twenty years Diane had minimal contact with her mother. She did not call her on the telephone, and she never sent a birthday card or a Mother's Day card. Nothing. Diane had moved several times and did not bother to give her mother her new address. It would be difficult if not impossible for her mother to find her, let alone communicate with her. No communication occurred between mother and daughter for almost two decades. During that time Diane found a job she enjoyed and also met someone whom she married.

One summer Diane and her husband hosted a difficult thirteen-year-old from the city. This young, distraught girl gave Diane a troublesome time. It did not take Diane long to realize that this was how she had treated her own mother. Now the shoe was on the other foot, although just for six weeks. That summer Diane realized how much her mother loved her to have put up with all her rebellion. For the first time she understood that her mother loved her despite everything she had done to upset her.

At the end of the summer Diane called her mother to thank her for loving her through some difficult times. It was the first time they had spoken in years. Diane told her mother, "I never realized how much you gave me and how hard it must have been for you." A mother-daughter relationship that had been strained for years and years was now beginning to heal, thanks in part to a mother who never stopped loving her daughter. The next weekend Diane and her husband went to visit with her mother. Diane and her mother stayed up all night, talking and crying.

Easter 7
John 17:1-11

The Cookout

"I glorified you on earth by finishing the work you gave me to do." (v. 4)

When Steve and Jan moved into their new home in a new neighborhood, it seemed like a dream come true. The surrounding houses were simply beautiful — each one was unique. The realtor told them that other young families lived in that suburban development. Obviously they were all affluent if they lived in such a lovely neighborhood.

Steve and Jan were delighted, almost bragging to their friends and family about their new home and their new neighborhood. Their street had finely manicured lawns, beautiful flower beds, and expensive cars in the driveways. They were indeed very fortunate to live where they did.

As summer approached Jan had an idea. She enthusiastically shared with her husband about having a neighborhood cookout. Jan wanted to invite all their new neighbors. It would be great fun and would also give them an opportunity to get to know their neighbors better. This was something they had not been able to do, still getting settled in their new home and new community. Steve agreed and a date was set. Early one Saturday morning Steve and Jan delivered the invitations to each neighbor's home. By week's end they were discouraged. Not one person said he or she would come. One couple said they were going away that weekend for a wedding, another said they were leaving for vacation that day. Some said they already had plans and were unable to attend. Some gave no excuse, saying only that they would not be attending. Some did not respond one way or the other.

Steve and Jan stayed up late that night trying to understand why no one responded to their invitation. As they talked they realized that none of the neighbors did anything social together. The neighbors see each other leave for work early in the morning, waving, occasionally saying hello, and then see them return home in the evening. On Saturday afternoons they might see one or two neighbors out mowing their lawns or taking a walk. That was it. That night Steve and Jan realized that the people in their neighborhood pretty much keep to themselves. Before going to bed, they agreed they would try again to host a get-together.

After three failed attempts to host a neighborhood cookout they finally persuaded their neighbors to agree on a date. To be honest, it took a lot of hard work for Jan and Steve to convince their new neighbors that this would be worthwhile.

The neighbors arrived that Saturday night. At first everyone was polite, making small talk about the weather, sports, or children. There were compliments about how nice their lawns looked. Some of the men began talking about cars. After everyone ate, the atmosphere changed as people were beginning to get to know each other better. The neighbors seemed to enjoy themselves and soon discovered common interests. Friendships were blossoming before the evening was over.

It was after midnight when the last of their guests left. All the neighbors said they had a great time, thanking Jan and Steve for making the get-together possible. More than one said they should do this more often.

They were exhausted but satisfied with the outcome. As they were busy cleaning up, Steve mentioned to Jan that he never thought it would be so difficult to bring the people in the neighborhood together.

Pentecost Sunday
Acts 2:1-21

A Gift Is Only A Gift When It Is Shared

But Peter, standing with the eleven, raised his voice and addressed them.... (v. 14a)

Beth cannot remember a time when she did not attend church, probably because she never had a choice. Her mother was the choir director, and later her older sister became the organist. Beth still attended the same church after she was married and had children. It was her church, after all, and she never thought of going to another church.

During a particularly stressful time in Beth's life she realized that the church could help her. At this point in her life she began paying closer attention to sermons and began reading the Bible. As a result, Beth's faith began to blossom. Beth's rekindled faith was alive and vital; it was taking on new meaning. She was not afraid to tell others about her new-found faith. Others in that church did not really understand the change that had taken place in her life; after all, they had known her and her family a long time.

Beth decided she wanted to lead the youth fellowship. Her own children would soon be old enough to attend and she wanted to make sure there was a youth fellowship for them. She put much time and energy into the youth program. For a small church they certainly had an excellent youth program with many creative lessons. Beth found that her faith continued to grow, and she was eager to continue learning and growing in her faith.

During her devotions one morning she happened across a Bible verse from Philippians: "I can do all things through him who strengthens me" (4:13). For some unknown reason that Bible verse stuck with her. It was almost as though the Lord kept reminding her, pushing her to believe it. She taught that Bible verse to her

Sunday School class and even talked to the youth about it. She adopted it; she wanted more than anything to live it.

A year later the pastor asked her if she would consider speaking on Mother's Day. The very notion of standing up in front of people scared her to death, even though this was her church and she knew everyone. She had never dreamed of doing such a thing. There was some tension between herself and the pastor so she did not want to say "no." Reluctantly she agreed to speak and began preparing a message. Beth kept thinking of that verse from Philippians, "I can do all things through him who strengthens me." Whenever fear gripped her she would think of that verse. She repeated that verse over and over in her mind. As she prepared her message she borrowed a commentary from the pastor and quickly gained new insight into the scriptures.

No one was more surprised than Beth that Sunday morning when she spoke. Beth discovered that she actually enjoyed speaking in church. Others in that congregation told her she had done a wonderful job. She felt good and soon recognized that she had a gift to share, the gift of speaking. Then Beth enrolled in a lay speaker course that summer. She would preach again at that church, and before too long at other churches. She felt called into the ministry and began taking courses and eventually was appointed part-time pastor of a small church.

A gift is only a gift when it is shared with the community of faith. "I never knew I had the gift," Beth says of her experience.

Could there be gifts you possess that you would be willing to share with others?

Trinity Sunday
Matthew 28:16-20

What No One Told Karen

"Go therefore and make disciples of all nations...." (v. 19a)

Like countless others of her generation, Karen grew up attending Sunday School and church and then completely dropped out during her teenage years. She returned to church in her mid-thirties, with children of her own. In some ways the experience of returning to church was like starting all over again. While she vaguely remembered some of the basics she learned long ago, much was new to her. Karen will admit that when she was a teenager she just was not interested, but now that she was older she wanted to learn and grow in her faith. It was refreshing to others in her Sunday School class to see how seriously she took the class. While others might have skipped reading the lessons, Karen always read them. Karen wanted to learn and grow. At first she was hesitant to ask questions for fear that she was asking "stupid questions." Others in the class encouraged her privately, telling her that they had the same questions but were too timid to ask them.

Karen began attending worship on a regular basis. Again she was familiar with the service while at the same time there was something new or different. Karen would literally sit on the edge of the pew listening. During the week she would ask her pastor questions as her faith continued to grow. She was encouraged to ask her questions.

The church emphasis was on "Inviting A Friend" to attend worship. While the pastor's words might have fallen on deaf ears, Karen took them seriously. Karen knew she had friends and neighbors who did not attend any church.

Karen offered to take her neighbors' children with her to Sunday School each week; she had plenty of room in her van. For several months Karen would bring a couple of neighborhood children to Sunday School with her. This was the first time the kids had ever been inside a church — much less attended Sunday School. The children went home singing songs and telling their parents about their lesson. When the women would get together for coffee Karen would tell them about the discussions from her Sunday School class the previous week. "You would really like our class," she told them.

Soon two of her neighbors began attending Sunday School and worshiping with her. The surprising thing was they fit right in with the class as if they had been attending for some time, thanks to Karen.

It might seem odd to some that Karen talks about matters of faith with her friends at the swimming pool or in her backyard. Karen has the God-given gift of sharing her faith in a way that is not threatening but rather inviting to others. In time it became apparent to others that Karen had a God-given gift of relating to other people. With encouragement Karen began using her gift.

Proper 5
Matthew 9:9-13, 18-26

"One Bodacious Party"

And as he sat at dinner in the house, many tax collectors and sinners came and were sitting with him and his disciples. (v. 10)

Doug enjoyed partying with his friends. All through his high school years he and his friends would have lots of fun partying on the weekends. They would go to one of their friend's home, preferably when his parents were away, and party. Beer was frequently involved in their partying. One of Doug's friends had an older brother who did not mind buying beer for his brother and his friends for a modest profit. Monday mornings at school Doug would brag to anyone who would listen, "I was like, totally wasted this weekend!" When asked for specific details he would honestly say he could not remember.

At graduation there was one all-night blow-out party. It was a fitting conclusion to high school for the police to come to quiet things down shortly after midnight. This would certainly be a party to remember. At various times during the summer Doug would say good-bye to his friends as they left for colleges in and out of state. By the end of the summer Doug was eager to start classes at the university.

Doug was like other freshmen at the university, and although he would probably never admit it, he was homesick — for his old friends and his family. His roommate was certainly different. Doug would observe his roommate reading a Bible or devotional material before going to bed every night. Doug did not know what to think of his roommate other than he would probably be stuck with him for a minimum of one semester, more than likely the whole school year. It's hard to explain what Doug was feeling, but he resented his roommate even though his roommate never said anything about religion to him. They were just different; they did not enjoy the same activities. Several weeks into the semester Doug decided to play a trick on his roommate and hide his Bible. Much to his surprise his roommate never said anything to him about it. Another time his roommate came back to the dorm to find his Bible with a leather belt tied around it as if to prevent him from reading it. Again his roommate said nothing about the incident.

Doug continued partying. He would often stumble back to his dorm room late at night, sometimes waking his roommate. His roommate never seemed to get mad at him, which surprised Doug. If the shoe were on the other foot Doug thought he would have had it out with his roommate by now. But Jeff was different.

Near the end of his first semester of college Doug and Jeff were studying in their room for finals. It was getting late and both would soon be going to sleep. Doug asked Jeff a question: "How do you keep so focused all the time? I mean, everything I do to disrupt you never seems to bother you." Jeff gave an honest response. The two young men stayed up another hour talking. Doug had plenty of questions for Jeff. Doug asked him why he read the Bible so much, admitting that he did not know anyone who ever read the Bible. It was an opportunity for faith dialogue. That night the seeds of faith were planted.

During Christmas break Doug went home. He had looked forward to being home with his family and friends for quite some time. Something seemed different to him. During the holiday his friends picked up where they had left off partying. Something just did not feel right to Doug. He went to the parties but felt awkward, as if he was out of place and did not belong there.

By the time the spring semester started, Doug looked forward to returning to class. He looked forward to speaking with Jeff, realizing that there was some quality about Jeff that he wanted in his own life. The second semester found Doug and Jeff hanging out more together. They went to basketball games together and shared other activities. Doug began attending Campus Fellowship meetings with Jeff. Once Doug was introduced to other Christians on campus he quickly made friends. He felt comfortable talking with other Christians, recognizing several from some of his classes. By the end of the semester Doug accepted Jesus Christ as his Lord and Savior.

It wasn't as through his roommate shoved religion down his throat. Doug first became friends with Jeff and saw how he lived. It was then that Doug realized that he wanted to emulate Jeff.

Proper 6
Genesis 18:1-15

The Visit

"I will surely return to you in due season, and your wife Sarah shall have a son." (v. 10a)

It was a "go nowhere" sort of a job. The job itself was fun, working part-time during high school. The extra spending money and the new friends made this job seem more than it actually was. This was not the sort of job one kept much past high school, working at a small fast food stand in the local mall. Once Joe graduated he worked full-time. He quickly realized that he should turn his attention in other directions. Joe's days were spent preparing food and waiting on customers.

Joe quickly made some new friends. When he worked part-time in the evening he knew other people; now that he was working full-time there were different people to meet. Workers of nearby stores would stop for a few minutes to talk. Joe was a friendly sort of a guy. One day a shopper stopped by explaining that it was her day to run errands. She had with her an elderly aunt and nearly blind uncle. She asked Joe how long he had worked there. She explained she usually shopped once a month and the next time she was in the mall she would stop to say hello. Joe was unsure what to think, a woman who appeared to be his mother's age with elderly relatives wanting to talk with him. Joe did not give this a second thought as he went about his work.

The next month, true to her word, the woman stopped by again with her aunt and uncle. She purchased sodas and stood sipping them while talking with Joe for a couple of minutes. She left, again saying she would see him next time she would be at the mall.

For the next several months this would be the woman's pattern. She would usually shop in mid-morning the second week of the month. Every time she would stop to talk she would have her elderly relatives with her. The woman did most of the talking while her aunt and uncle just stood by quietly sipping their drinks or eating their snacks. Joe enjoyed visiting a few minutes with this pleasant woman every month.

Joe never mentioned anything about being dissatisfied with his job. By summer's end he realized he should be doing more with his life. The monotony of doing the exact same thing day in and day out was getting to Joe. Joe thought about going to college and began writing to several colleges for information.

One day as the woman was visiting with Joe she said something very profound. She told Joe he would make a good pastor. That was all she said. Joe had never spoken of the longing in his heart. This woman saw something in Joe that he was actually contemplating. For Joe it was a moment of divine affirmation. Having said that, the woman left. Joe began college classes that January. Joe does not remember ever talking with this woman again.

Proper 7
Matthew 10:24-39

Noelle's Summer Vacation

"Those who find their life will lose it, and those who lose their life for my sake will find it." (v. 39)

Noelle was an attractive strawberry blond who grew up in southern California. She enjoyed being out of doors in the fresh air. She spent her summers on the beach with the sun beating down on her. She never seemed to tire of being at the beach. She always had a great tan. Noelle was very popular, having many friends.

She chose a college in southern California, because she did not want to be too far from the beach. While at college Noelle made friends with people from other parts of the country. Her new friends were different from her old friends; it took her several months to realize how they were different. Her new friends had a strong faith. Her friends told of how they wanted to help other people, an idea that was totally foreign to Noelle. She never gave much thought to faith either. She was always amused at stories in magazines or on the evening news where people claimed that their faith made a difference in their lives. "Yea, right," she would think to herself. Noelle would be hard pressed to name any of her high school friends who even attended church. "None of my friends back home did the church scene," she explained.

While she was not sure of her faith, she did want to help other people. Her new friends' enthusiasm was contagious. So the summer after her second year of college found Noelle and several of her friends living in Camden, New Jersey, in one of the worst neighborhoods in the United States. The area where she spent the summer had one of the highest crime rates in the country. Violence would erupt over seemingly nothing at any time of the day or night. It was a neighborhood where it was never safe to walk the streets alone, day or night. She vividly recalled being shocked by what she saw the first day as she and her friends drove to the place where they would live. Across the street, a liquor store drew a steady stream of drunks, drug dealers, and prostitutes. There was graffiti blanketed across every wall within sight. That first day she wondered what in the world she had gotten herself into.

Noelle explained why she volunteered to live among the poorest people in the nation: "I feel like I was just really blessed, and I wanted to give something back." She had nothing in common with the youth she wanted to work with; a couple of them even made fun of her southern California accent.

That summer she persuaded one teenager to give up his gun and stop dealing drugs. There were times that she felt like giving up, but she kept plugging away. One night Noelle showed up at the youth center with a roll of brown paper and markers, hoping the group would draw a mural. At first only two boys showed up. Others stood around in the back of the room mocking her. She paid no attention to them and continued. Gradually, one by one, some of the others began gathering around the table.

That night as the youth left, one troubled teenage girl remained and spent the next two hours talking with Noelle. This fourteen-year-old girl had experienced more than her share of heartache and problems in her young life. Noelle listened and offered words of hope, encouraging her to make some needed changes in her life.

Noelle and the other young people were able to offer the inner city teenagers something they had never had before — hope. This would be an experience Noelle and her friends would never forget. They made a difference in other people's lives and in the process they were also touched. Noelle came to faith on her own during her last year of college.

Proper 8
Matthew 10:40-42

God's Direction

"Whoever welcomes you welcomes me, and whoever welcomes me welcomes the one who sent me." (v. 40)

If it's true that our family of origin defines who we are from the moment of our birth, then Marvin is a shining example. Marvin is the youngest of three children; both his older sisters were born with severe mental retardation. Marvin says that when his sisters were born in the mid-1950s the family doctor instructed his parents immediately to send the girls to an institution where they could be cared for. The doctor also told his parents that they should not have any more children. "It's a good thing," Marvin says with a chuckle, "Mom and Dad did not listen or I would not be here."

Marvin remembers his early years in school when his classmates would make fun of students with learning disabilities and other handicapping conditions. "They were so cruel." He would feel bad for those children being made fun of by others. For this reason he was hesitant to bring friends to his home. He was afraid to tell his friends about his sisters or they might think something was wrong with him and begin making fun of him. One weekend each month Marvin and his parents would travel two hundred miles, to the other end of the state, to visit his sisters. "We did this for years," he says.

As a young person Marvin was searching for what God wanted him to do with his life. He always enjoyed being around people. It was no surprise to anyone who knew him that his first job was driving a school bus. He enjoyed interacting with the students on a daily basis. The students thought he was funny and would joke with him. During this time he also worked as a carpenter at his father's shop. Five years later Marvin felt God calling him in another direction, so he quit both of his jobs and enrolled in a Bible college in one of the western states. He admits one of the reasons was that the college catalog had pictures of students back-packing through the Rocky Mountains. "I thought it would be fun," Marvin explains.

One year later Marvin was back home, where he enrolled in a nearby Bible college. Upon graduation Marvin served as pastor of a small church for six years. Again his love for people shined through everything he did. Somewhere deep inside he felt that God wanted him to do something else with his life.

One day, out of the blue, someone called asking if he would be interested in being the director of a halfway house for the mentally challenged. The person explained that the people living at these homes, throughout the county, held jobs during the day. They needed supervision and group activities during the evenings and on weekends. There were some who required more care. Marvin prayed about this opportunity. With the support of his family, he accepted the position.

Marvin has a real passion for helping the mentally challenged. It is obvious how much he loves them. When he speaks at service clubs Marvin always brings one of the residents with him, introducing the resident and allowing the person to say a few words to the group. Each week he leads worship, encouraging residents to participate. Marvin always treats the residents as children of God who are of great value to God, as they are for him.

With a sense of certainty Marvin says, "This is what God wants me to do."

Proper 9
Matthew 11:16-19, 25-30

Ida's Attic

"Take my yoke upon you, and learn from me; for I am gentle and humble in heart, and you will find rest for your souls." (v. 29)

What drew people to Ida was her cheerfulness. She was always happy and always had something nice to say to everyone she met. Children felt comfortable talking with the "nice lady" at church. Young adults looked up to Ida as an example, often going out of their way to do something extra special for her.

Ida was young at heart. That was how some of the people at church described her. Her advancing years were beginning to catch up with her, slowing her down. Ida has lived alone ever since her husband died almost five years ago.

The family had been discussing the possibility of Ida going to live in a retirement community. Ida was an independent woman who tried her best to convince her family that she was perfectly all right living in her home. After all, she told them, her house had been her home for nearly sixty years. After much debate and protesting it was decided that Ida would go to live in the retirement home. She would have people to look after her around the clock, her daughter told her. Ida did not want to hear that but knew it was no use arguing. Perhaps deep down she knew her daughter was probably right and she would be better off living in a retirement community instead of by herself.

Some of the women from her church volunteered to help clean her house in preparation for a public sale some six weeks away. Ida welcomed their help. In those last weeks in her own home Ida had many decisions to make. What should she take with her, and what should she give away to her family? She remembered one of her granddaughters always admired one of her rings, while one of her grandsons wanted the railroad spike her husband proudly talked about every time the grandchildren came to visit. Then there were the items to try to sell. There were some things that would need to be thrown away. While cleaning out her house Ida found marvelous things she had not seen or thought of for many years. She found so many wonderful things, old postcards and pictures, mementos of her long life and the many places she and her husband had visited. Finding such treasures slowed down the process as Ida would call the women and tell a story about the object she found. "That picture was taken in 1943 when we visited my oldest brother in New York," Ida explained. Another picture showed Ida and her husband standing in an orange grove. "Years ago when we went to Florida one winter we met the nicest man who owned an orange grove," she told the women. "He let us pick our own oranges and sent us some oranges for Christmas." Some afternoons very little work was accomplished, but no one seemed to mind.

The women helping Ida saw a side of her they had never seen before as she openly began talking about her life. The women did not know about all her struggles. They saw a happy, friendly woman who always had nice things to say. In the weeks of cleaning Ida's house she never once said, "I wish I had done something else with my life." Ida had no regrets even though her life was filled with plenty of ups and downs. When asked about her faith she would say, "I put my trust in God and will not concern myself with what might have been!"

Proper 10
Matthew 13:1-9, 18-23

Seventh Grade Sunday School Class

"Other seeds fell on good soil and brought forth grain, some a hundredfold, some sixty, some thirty." (v. 8)

Hank and Charlene were gifted Sunday School teachers. They were the teachers for the seventh grade class. Most weeks they would have close to twenty students. It was not easy to think of lessons and activities that would hold the interest of seventh graders. But they were dedicated. As Charlene explained, "Seventh grade is such an important grade for the kids."

It was obvious that much time went into teaching the class. Their lesson plans included new and creative teaching methods. Hank and Charlene used hands-on learning methods before they became popular. One Sunday all the tables were rearranged; the center table was set for a Seder meal complete with bitter herbs and matzo. The symbolism was explained as the class experienced the Seder meal as Jewish families have for centuries. Another Sunday the class painted large cardboard boxes, making them ships. "The church is like a ship," Hank explained as the students were busy painting. Another Sunday there was a discussion on finding ways to live out their Christian life. Charlene told of how Christians from other times lived out their lives for the Lord. Hank had the students look up and read verses from the Bible.

No one remembers what happened one Sunday near the end of the school year. What is remembered is that the class quickly got out of hand. There were disruptive comments, there was laughter, and no one seemed to be paying the least attention. Were the students tired of Sunday School? Maybe they were just being seventh graders. Finally Hank had had enough. For the first time he spoke harsh words, revealing his frustration. "You know," he began, "we spend a lot of time preparing for this class. If this is how you are going to treat us — you can just find other teachers." Charlene said nothing, but it was apparent she too was upset.

The class sat there in total silence, too stunned to say anything. Being seventh graders, they did not know what to say. They might not have admitted it, but they really enjoyed their class and certainly liked their teachers. When the bell rang the students breathed a sigh of relief.

The next September there were new teachers for this class. By the time they graduated from high school over half the class would no longer attend either church or Sunday School. However, Hank and Charlene would be pleased to know that some of the seeds they planted in these young people did germinate and take root. Twenty-five years later, several members of that class are still very active in their church. Several have taught Sunday School classes, while others have tried their hand at leading a youth fellowship. Another class member chaired the church's official board for several years. These adults have their seventh grade Sunday School teachers to thank for making the gospel relevant for them. Much to their regret, they never had the opportunity to thank Hank and Charlene.

Proper 11
Matthew 13:24-30, 36-43

And Then There Was Eve

"Master ... where, then did these weeds come from?" (v. 28b)

Eve was one of those kids who, no matter how hard anyone tried, no one could reach. What made it so difficult was her defiant, rebellious spirit. She dressed in outrageous clothing that signaled, "I like being different." Once she even dyed her hair a deep purple. She had a mean streak and would often pick on other students, belittling them in class. Parents would warn their children to stay clear of Eve in hopes that they would not turn out like her. She wasn't always like this but once she started junior high school she took a change for the worse.

Eve always tried her best to disrupt her Sunday School class by continuing to change the subject. In class she seldom allowed the teacher to remain on one subject for too long or complete a lesson. It was hard to keep Eve silent; some of the other kids called her "motor mouth." One Sunday School teacher quit teaching because of Eve. Another quit teaching when she learned that Eve would be in her class that fall. She knew all about Eve from the other teachers. Eve was that kind of child. When Sunday School teachers would talk together they all had stories to tell about Eve. "She will never change." "She is just no good — plain and simple," they would say. "She will never amount to anything." A couple of teachers even said out loud that they wished that Eve would stop attending Sunday School. "We don't need that sort of person in our Sunday School program."

Ted agreed to teach the junior high class that fall. He was a school teacher and was familiar with the uniqueness of junior high students. Some of the other teachers tried their best to warn Ted about Eve, but he seemed to pay little attention to them. "I can handle the situation," he assured the concerned persons. "I deal with junior high students every day." At their first class together Eve was her loud, disruptive self. She was pushing her limits to see how much she could get away with before the new teacher became angry. Ted would later admit that he never met a student quite like Eve. "She is a challenge," he said with a grin.

As the year progressed Ted made it a point to get to know Eve better. He found out what music she enjoyed and gave her discs to listen to at home. Before youth fellowship Ted would ask Eve what she liked about a particular song and they would talk about it for several minutes. Ted helped Eve with a school project when her parents were just too busy to help her. As the year progressed Eve began to change. She began to soften up. The first sign of her change was that she stopped wearing outrageous clothing. She no longer felt it was necessary to make fun of other students in the mean-spirited way she had before. She even began paying attention to the lesson.

What made the difference in Eve, the child no one was able to reach? It was the loving attitude of Ted who viewed her as a precious child of God.

Proper 12
Romans 8:26-39

Alice's Hindsight

We know that all things work together for good for those who love God, who are called according to his purpose. (v. 28)

Alice would be the first to admit that she was too young when she got married. She had two children before she realized she had made a terrible mistake. Like many young women she held romantic visions of what marriage would be like. She thought her life would be different, wonderful somehow. Instead her husband was, well, let's just say inattentive to her needs. It took all the courage and strength she had to leave her husband but she realized she had to for her own peace of mind. Life was anything but easy for a divorced mother with two young children. She was the first person in her extended family to be divorced. Besides all the pain that comes from a break-up of a marriage she felt additional pain as some of her friends kept their distance. Even in her church, the church she grew up in, the only church she had ever attended, she felt rejected. Alice had a difficult time for a long while.

During her time of struggle Alice's faith was rekindled. She had attended church all her life, but for some reason her faith never really clicked. As her young children approached school age she met a wonderful Christian man whom she would eventually marry. For the first time in a long time Alice was happy. Alice had a passion to share her faith with others in her community, especially the young people. This was her personal mission to help others avoid what she went through. She started teaching Sunday School and before too long was leading the youth fellowship on Sunday evenings.

Alice continued growing in her faith as she taught and led the youth. She had questions to ask, hoping that her pastor could answer. One day she asked her pastor if he believed God brought people together in relationships. The pastor was too quick with his answer. "No," he told her as he went on to explain that people meet each other randomly, often through circumstance. Alice was disappointed in his answer. She had hoped he would have said yes because that was how she felt — that God had brought her and her husband together.

One evening Alice was speaking with her youth fellowship when she shared her favorite scripture passage. The Bible verses that meant the most to her in her faith walk were found in Romans 8, she told the teenagers as she read. It was an authentic moment as Alice spoke of her faith in the deep conviction that no matter what happened in her life that God was there, never deserting her. She did not always understand why she had to experience some difficult times, but now that she looked back she could see the Lord helping her though her worst days. She only spoke for a couple of minutes. She hoped that if there was one thing these youth would remember it was what she had just said.

Proper 13
Matthew 14:13-21

Aunt Betty's Advice

"They need not go away; you give them something to eat."
(v. 16)

On a warm August afternoon a large extended family gathered for a family reunion. Family get-togethers were an annual event years ago, when the grandparents were living. Now it was once or twice every decade or so. On this particular afternoon, the family met on a farm, complete with a pond and barn. Some of the cousins had not seen each other in twenty years. It did not take too long for the cousins to catch up on what was happening in each others' lives. "You must be Mike," one of the cousins said. "The last time I saw you — I do not think you were ten years old," one of the older relatives said. There were introductions of spouses and young children that afternoon. There were even some re-introductions just in case someone might have forgotten. "You remember Dave's wife, Dawn. You met at their wedding." The first hour or so all one heard was, "I can't believe how much you have grown — the last time I saw you...."

What made this family reunion so special was having Aunt Betty and her son, Jim, present. Aunt Betty was a special woman who had lived most of her life in Alaska, far away from the rest of the family. There was a twinkle in Aunt Betty's eye as she took time to greet each niece and nephew and their families, many of whom she was meeting for the first time. "I'm so glad you could come," she would say as she embraced each family member. "There's nothing like being a part of a family. Oh, you can have friends," she continued, "and friends can be helpful but there's nothing like family to support you." With that she would go and greet another relative. It was obvious that she had missed her family.

There were plenty of smiles and laughter that afternoon. By evening the family shared a meal together. Each family brought food to share. With paper plates everyone stood in line waiting for the food, making small talk with other relatives. Second cousins twice removed sat next to newly discovered third cousins. As they filled their plates and sat down there was silence in that yard, a silence that could not be intruded upon. They were a large, extended family. Even though this extended family seldom had seen each other they were still a part of the family — connected in a bond that can never be broken.

Sharing a meal together cemented an invisible bond that held this family together.

Proper 14
Matthew 14:22-33

Roller Coaster Ride

But when he noticed the strong wind, he became frightened, and beginning to sink, he cried out, "Lord, save me!" (v. 30)

Rob was like any other teenager; he enjoyed doing the usual things that teenagers do. During school Rob and his friends would hang out after school. On the weekends they would spend several hours walking around the mall. They did not do much, they just liked being together. The week after school was out his friends had talked about spending a day at an amusement park several hours away. They had talked about this before but never were able to agree on a date. They set a date for August. They would have a great time together. There were a couple of new rides that were being advertised as "totally awesome" that they could hardly wait to try out. Rob was reluctant to go. He did not want to sound like a wimp but he really did not like amusement parks. He had a deathly fear of high, fast-moving thrill rides. Rob wasn't sure where this fear came from, he never had any bad experiences. He just did not like heights combined with speed. His friends knew nothing about his fear of fast-moving thrill rides.

With much convincing Rob finally agreed to go with his friends. While his friends went on one ride after another Rob waited patiently for them on the ground. He watched as his friends rode each ride, laughing and obviously having a great time. Confidentially, he wished he could have fun with his friends. He felt that he was missing out on something, but he just could not bring himself to get on those scary rides. Rob was certain that he would not like the rides his friends were enjoying. He did not like heights, he did not like fast-moving rides, he did not want to be frightened. At first no one seemed to notice that Rob was not having a good time.

By early afternoon one of his friends said, "Go on this ride with us." His friends promised to go with him, assuring him that he would not in any way be injured. Perhaps it was peer pressure, but Rob caved in and agreed to ride the roller coaster — just once. His friends accompanied him up the steps while Rob kept saying over and over, "I can't believe I'm doing this — I just know I'm not going to like it."

As the roller coaster climbed upward, Rob was afraid to look down. When the other kids on the ride were screaming, raising their arms high as the roller coaster plunged, Rob was holding on for dear life, his hands firmly gripping the safety bar. Later he admitted that he closed his eyes for most of the ride.

When the ride was finally over, Rob felt something he never felt before — exhilaration. He felt more alive than ever. He was smiling, obviously enjoying the moment. He felt safe and secure. Rob was the first one to get back in line for a second ride. If only he had tried this sooner.

Proper 15
Matthew 15:21-28

Carla's Persistence

Then Jesus answered her, "Woman, great is your faith! Let it be done for you as you wish." (v. 28)

Carla was a fighter. That much was evident from several telephone conversations. The church secretary asked the preschool teacher who this woman was who kept calling. "She is very demanding," the teacher replied with a laugh. Carla wanted her daughter to attend a preschool, sponsored by the church. Carla's daughter, Kristal, was born with spina-bifida, a rare disease that affects the back. Kristal was fragile; just by falling on the floor she could break her leg or hip. She had spent much of her young life in a body cast. It was for this reason that several other preschools were reluctant to accept Kristal in their programs. "For most parents," Carla said, "this is an exciting and emotional experience. A time for letting go so that our child can learn, grow, and achieve." Carla wanted her daughter to have the same opportunities other children her age had.

Carla described her experience as a nightmare. "I found that no one was prepared to hear the word, 'handicapped.'" They were so discreet at first that Carla did not realize that discrimination was taking place. There were excuses she kept hearing, about a school being too active, or having steps, or having to gain permission from the governing board.

"I was determined not to give up," Carla says. She was certainly persistent. After an exhausting search she found one preschool director who was willing to meet with her. Carla was willing to do just about anything to have Kristal in preschool. She checked with the insurance company to make sure her daughter would be covered. She contacted an agency to arrange for a full-time aide to stay with Kristal during preschool. She did not care

— she just wanted her daughter to experience what other kids her age experienced.

Carla was happy when she received the news she wanted to hear: Kristal would be attending preschool. Kristal is a beautiful, delightful, intelligent four-year-old girl, who was able to walk with the aid of a walker, while sometimes riding in a wheelchair. The first day of school Kristal was wearing a new blue dress. She looked so beautiful. Carla was so happy. As the school year progressed it was a real joy to have Kristal in the preschool program.

The reason for Carla's persistence soon became evident. Carla knew firsthand what it meant to live with a handicapping condition. She knew what her daughter would encounter from the other children: the stares, the insensitive remarks she would likely endure, and the distance others would keep. Through her own experience Carla had learned to be a fighter. She had to fight for everything she wanted, and she was certainly going to fight for her daughter, hoping that she could make life easier for her daughter.

The preschool director might have been hesitant at first but once Kristal was in class she knew she had made the right decision. Kristal got along fine with the other children and soon made many new friends. By the end of the school year other children showed a real concern for Kristal.

"My advice to parents with 'special children' is, don't give up!" Carla proudly stated.

Proper 16
Romans 12:1-8

Rally Day

For by the grace given to me I say to everyone among you not to think of yourself more highly than you ought to think, but to think with sober judgment, each according to the measure of faith that God has assigned. (v. 3)

Plans for Rally Day were discussed at the Sunday School teachers meeting. At the meeting Jay mentioned that many in the congregation had never toured the Sunday School department. Someone else said she felt there was very little interest in the teaching ministry of the church from the congregation at large. Others nodded their heads in agreement. After much idea sharing it was decided to hold an open house on Rally Day. They would invite the entire congregation, not just those with children, to visit the Sunday School classrooms. The children would make invitations and then personally hand them to adults. They would also make posters and hang them in the halls. Someone suggested that maybe the children should lead the adults by the hand to their classrooms. There were some chuckles but also an element of truth in the statement. It was hard to get the congregation excited about Sunday School. It was a great meeting with everyone's enthusiasm running high. This would be a great Rally Day.

Just before the meeting ended, Bob, one of the more seasoned Sunday School teachers, voiced his opinion. He explained that he did not want to put a damper on everyone's obvious enthusiasm, "but I've been around long enough to know," he said. "People just are not interested enough to come to see the Sunday School classes. Frankly," he stated in a matter of fact tone, "I do not see any more adults coming than in previous years."

There was silence as a cloud of gloom seemed to descend on everyone. The enthusiasm the group had experienced a few minutes earlier was suddenly drained. After what seemed like an eternity the Sunday School superintendent, Twila, who was both new to the church and position, said she was willing to try the new idea. She explained that she felt it would work and it was worth trying. Several other Sunday School teachers agreed with her, even though they realized that Bob's words contained an element of truth.

Several weeks later on Rally Day the children went to the worship center and invited adults to their classrooms, leading them in some cases by the hand. All along the hall were colorful posters and helium-filled balloons. The children were proud of their projects.

Rally Day was a great success. Adults in the congregation who did not participate in the Sunday School realized how important the Sunday School was to their church. They experienced firsthand the children's excitement. Rally Day touched some in unexpected ways. One person offered to buy tape recorders for each classroom; others volunteered to help out with teaching or other special events. It was truly a great day to kick off another year of Sunday School.

Proper 17
Exodus 3:1-15

Janice And The Bulldozer

"So come, I will send you to Pharaoh to bring my people, the Israelites, out of Egypt." (v. 10)

    The picture in the evening newspaper would certainly catch anyone's attention: three women sitting on a blanket in the foreground, a fresh mound of dirt on the left, a bulldozer raring to go on the right. The article told how the young mothers were protesting the construction of a new school. They felt it was wrong to develop farm land for yet another school that in their opinion was unneeded. These mothers felt the new school would place an unfair burden on the homeowners.

    One of the women, Janice, was convinced it was wrong. She wanted to do something to stop the construction. After talking with various school and township officials and getting nowhere, she realized the only way to halt the work was to place herself in harm's way. Maybe then people would listen. She wanted others to hear what she had to say instead of allowing the school district to do whatever it pleased. Janice and two of her friends spent the day at the construction sight. They even brought their lunches. Their presence prevented any work from being done that day.

    There was an ugly confrontation between the construction workers and these three women. There was a strife between school officials and the women. The police were called to arrest these women. The women would not move, vowing to come back the next day and the next. They would do whatever it took to stop the construction. A newspaper reporter and photographer came to recount the events of the day. Janice hoped the publicity would create public support for her point of view. While the mothers did gain attention for their cause, the new school was built on schedule.

For Janice this was just the beginning of her community involvement. She started attending school board meetings. While school board members wished they could find a way to keep this woman quiet or, better yet, to stop attending their meetings, she kept coming. She would raise her concerns at the meetings; she would question the school's budget and the amount they proposed to spend on extra-curricular activities. She said over and over again that she wanted the school district to act more responsibly for the good of the community and its students. Janice would have her picture in the newspaper again, this time standing before the school board sharing one of her concerns.

Her friends encouraged her to run for the school board at the next election. Janice ran, promising to be the voice of the common person. She lost that election. In many ways Janice was ahead of her time. She ran a second time and this time she won the election.

For over twenty years, long after her children graduated, Janice has served on the school board. As time went on she won the respect of others in her community. Janice was admired for both her courage and honesty as she spoke on behalf of others.

Proper 18
Romans 13:8-14

The Defining Mark

Owe no one anything, except to love one another; for the one who loves another has fulfilled the law. (v. 8)

Rollin and Tom were colleagues at a small Christian college. Both were esteemed professors, one teaching the New Testament and the other family counseling. Their relationship at best was distant. They would say "hello" to each other when they passed in the hall or at staff meetings, but that was the extent of their relationship. They were friendly toward each other but did not consider themselves friends. On important issues Rollin and Tom were on opposing sides, often at odds with each other.

It just so happened that Rollin and Tom were attending a seminar in New York City. Of course they traveled separately even though they would be staying at the same hotel. Shortly after dinner Tom became violently ill. He made it as far as the men's room before collapsing. He would later claim it was something he ate that did not agree with him. What he actually said was he suffered from food poisoning. When Rollin saw what had happened to Tom he took him to his hotel room. Rollin helped Tom into bed and called the front desk to find out if there might be a doctor on call. An hour later the doctor arrived and prescribed medicine. The doctor instructed Tom to stay in bed and get as much rest as he could for the next 24 hours. Most importantly, he was not to attempt to eat anything although it was important to keep his fluid levels up.

Rollin would stay at Tom's side, taking good care of him. He telephoned Tom's spouse to inform her that her husband was sick but he would be all right. He notified the person in charge of the seminar of Tom's condition, as well as the Dean back home. Throughout the night whenever Tom needed help, Rollin was there.

The next morning Tom felt much better but was very weak. Rollin found a store and bought him some ginger ale. Rollin did not leave Tom's side until he was certain that he would be all right.

Later Tom would tell one of his classes that he never would have volunteered or desired to room or even travel with Rollin. He would never have thought of going out to dinner with Rollin and his wife or doing anything social with them. But that night in the hotel room he saw a side of Rollin he had never seen before. Even though they might not have been friends they were united as Christians. Tom experienced love in action. That night when he was so sick Rollin was there with him, helping him through a very unpleasant situation. Tom was glad Rollin was there. There would be times when these two professors would find themselves on opposing sides, but deep down they were on the same side — they were Christians who lived out their convictions.

Proper 19
Romans 14:1-12

Amber's Stand

It is before their own lord that they stand or fall. And they will be upheld, for the Lord is able to make them stand. (4b)

Amber was thrilled when she made the girl's varsity basketball team in her junior year of high school. She really loved basketball and practiced hard to make the team.

Amber was encouraged by fellow teammates and her parents. Her coach told her that with a couple of good years she would be able to receive scholarships to any number of colleges with good basketball programs. This became Amber's goal. She would practice and play hard with the hope of receiving a scholarship. Her parents always told her to dream the impossible dream, which she did.

Amber was also very active in her church's youth group. She helped plan a weekend retreat with other youth from several area churches. It would be a great weekend together in the mountains. Not only would there be plenty to do that weekend, but Amber also saw it as a chance to grow in her faith. Amber's parents paid the deposit to ensure she would go. Amber did not think too much about it; the retreat would take place a couple of weeks after basketball season was completed. The youth were eagerly anticipating their retreat, talking about it at practically every meeting.

It was one of those unforgettable seasons for the girls' basketball team. They did better than anyone had honestly expected. Amber was among the team's leading scorers. The team not only had a winning record, but they would also be in the state playoffs for the first time ever. A sports writer for the local newspaper wrote that the team had a very good chance to win the state championship. All the girls on the team were ecstatic.

As the girls were practicing for the playoffs Amber realized that one of the games was scheduled for the same weekend as her church youth group retreat. She knew her team needed her while at the same time she really wanted to go on the retreat with the other youth. Her parents told her it was her decision to make. Either she would play basketball or she would go with the youth group on their retreat. This was not an easy decision to make, but Amber made her own choice. First, she told her parents, then the youth group, and finally her coach. She would not play basketball but would instead go on the weekend retreat with her church youth group. Her parents were so proud of her. They did not have to tell her what to do or what was more important. She had made her own decision.

The coach was a completely different story. She told Amber that if she wasn't going to participate in that one playoff game she would let her teammates down and would be off the team. Not only would she be off the team, the coach told her, she would seriously jeopardize any future college scholarships she might receive.

While many might have caved in to the pressure, Amber did not. She went with her youth group and had a fantastic weekend at the retreat.

Proper 20
Matthew 20:1-16

Ed's Vacation

"Am I not allowed to do what I choose with what belongs to me? Or are you envious because I am generous?" (v. 15)

Ed and Darlene were looking forward to their summer vacation. They were fortunate to find reasonable rates at an exclusive resort area that they had never been to before and in all probability would never be able to visit again. They were thrilled with the opportunity.

"Now we will see how the other half lives," Darlene told Ed once the reservations were made. New clothing was bought. "We want to look nice and fit in," Darlene reasoned. Together they read the tour book, finding the family restaurants, golf courses, and other places of interest that the whole family would enjoy. They studied the hotel brochure. The kids were excited about the indoor and outdoor pool as well as the health club. In looking over the brochure they knew they had never stayed anywhere quite so nice.

The day arrived to leave for vacation. Ed and Darlene left on their dream vacation. It would be a long day driving, but it would be well worth it once they arrived at their destination. The kids were even excited.

Upon arriving they stopped at the Welcome Center. Ed always likes to stop to pick up sightseeing information as well as the occasional discount coupon for area sights and restaurants.

As they were leaving the Welcome Center, brochures in hand, they encountered a group of people handing out blue papers. Ed took one, politely thanking the person. Several hours later, after checking into the resort, Ed was reading the information he had picked up at the Welcome Center and found the blue piece of paper.

What he read disturbed him. Darlene told him simply to throw the paper away and forget it. "We're on vacation now," she told him. Ed could not.

This resort community, a favorite retirement area as well as a vacation destination, paid workers less than the minimum wage. It did not seem right to Ed. Some of the wealthiest people in the region lived there year round; other well-off people vacationed there, while just several miles inland lived some of the poorest people in the state. The paper encouraged vacationers to leave tips for the workers, many of whom were living in or near poverty. Ed was appalled. How could people so well off treat other people so badly?

Not only did Ed tip the workers he encountered in the couple of days he vacationed there, but he also found the addresses of state and local government officials to whom he would write once they returned home. Ed knew it just wasn't right. Something had to be done to help the workers, and he was willing to do all he could.

Proper 21
Matthew 21:23-32

Two Brothers

"Which of the two did the will of his father?" (v. 31a)

Bobby and his brother Gordie were waiting to be picked up to attend Vacation Bible School at their neighborhood church. As they were patiently waiting, one of Gordie's friends happened by and began making fun of him. "You have to go," his friend taunted, "and I don't."

While Bobby paid no attention, Gordie took the matter to heart. Gordie felt bad and wished he did not have to go. He wanted to stay home with his friends. This became a defining moment for Gordie who would put up quite a fight each Sunday. He did not want to go to Sunday School and church. His parents told Gordie he not only had to go but he had no choice in the matter. One Sunday they were about half way to church when Gordie announced that he was sick, so sick that he would be throwing up any minute. Immediately the car was turned around and home they went. Of course, once Gordie was home he felt much better. He wasn't really sick. It was just an excuse. On another occasion Gordie went to church with his brother and parents but, unknown to them, he left through another door. He spent the entire time sitting by himself in the car. Anything was better than having to sit through a boring Sunday School class he wanted no part of.

It was hard for some in the church to believe that Bobby and Gordie were brothers. Bobby never put up a fight. He took pleasure in attending Sunday School and was disappointed the weeks he could not attend, thanks to Gordie. Bobby would get mad at his brother when he faked an illness.

As the boys grew, the tension between them continued, as did their like and dislike of church and Sunday School. By the time Gordie was in middle school he completely dropped out of Sunday

School and church. His parents were tired of fighting him week after week. It was easier to leave him home by himself. At least now his parents could enjoy worship without having to fight Gordie every week.

The years passed with little change in attitude with Bobby and Gordie. Bobby continued attending Sunday School and church, and as a young adult he began teaching a class. His brother Gordie, on the other hand, never set foot inside the church.

Ten years later Gordie began attending a church that had a contemporary worship service, complete with a "praise band." Later he enrolled in an in-depth Bible study. The atmosphere was different at this church than at the church he had attended as a child. For the first time in Gordie's life he was both interested and open to the church.

The ten years did not fare quite as well with Bobby. While he was active in the church into his twenties, by his late twenties he had completely dropped out of the life of the church. He did not tell anyone; he just stopped teaching, serving on committees and attending church. He could not give a reason and no one asked. He just stopped attending. When Gordie questioned him, the only thing Bobby could say was that he was disillusioned about the whole concept of God and the church. "Why go if it doesn't mean anything?" Bobby rationalized. These two brothers were different, all right.

Proper 22
Matthew 21:33-46

Missed Out

Have you never read in the scriptures: "The stone that the builders rejected has become the cornerstone...." (v. 42)

Have you ever missed an opportunity that you were later sorry you neglected to act on? That was Barry's experience. When Barry was in the seventh grade he missed an opportunity. All the seventh graders were required to take a typing class for half the year. As a seventh grader, Barry thought, "Why in the world do I need to learn how to type?" He saw no practical use whatsoever to learn how to type. He did not take the class as seriously as he should have. Barry knew his father had his own secretary and she typed all his correspondence. Why would he need to learn how to type? he rationalized to his parents. By Barry's own admission, "I goofed off in class, sometimes giving the teacher a hard time."

The newly completed middle school had a typing lab complete with manual typewriters for each student. When everyone in the class finished typing one line a bell would ring. The class would be typing and all the bells would ring at the same time — that is, except for Barry's. It became a game for him. His bell would ring at times before the rest of the class. The class would be typing along and then Barry's bell would ring, and he would start laughing. He did this on purpose. He thought it was funny. It was obvious to the teacher that Barry was making little or no effort in learning how to type and was distracting the other students who wanted to learn. When he did actually try to type he would look at the keys so the teacher had to cover them with masking tape. He would have to learn the location of the keys. Then there was that lunch period that he spent in the typing lab, practicing typing.

It was no great surprise to anyone that at the end of the semester Barry did not know how to type. He did not receive a passing grade either. He was finished with typing forever — at least that was what he thought at the time.

Today Barry will be the first to admit that he has paid dearly for his short-sightedness. Several years later in college he had to both beg and pay people to type his term papers. As a seventh grader he never would have dreamed that one day there would be computers and word processors and that it would be a benefit to know how to type. The day came when everyone in his office had their own personal computers, and Barry was expected to know how to use his. Barry would be passed over for several promotions all because he could not type.

Barry was nearly thirty years old when he finally learned how to type. He bought typing books and tapes to learn how to type in his free time, something he should have learned years before.

Proper 23
Matthew 22:1-14

Not At My Church!

And he said to him, "Friend, how did you get in here without a wedding robe?" And he was speechless. (v. 12)

For years George had been complaining that the attendance was down at the church he had attended all his life. "I do not ever remember it being so low," he complained one evening at the church board meeting. "Just several years ago we would have close to a hundred people at worship every week," he said. "Now we have trouble reaching a hundred on Easter Sunday." There were others that agreed with George. They too noticed the steady decline in worship attendance over the years. There were some who remembered the good old days when everyone in the community went to church. "When Pastor Wonderful was our pastor," Thelma told the group, "our church was full every Sunday." Others at the meeting began to place the blame on external things, like some of the policies of the denomination. Then there was that church with the new, modern building on the outskirts of town that played guitars during its worship services.

Rod sat there listening to what everyone said, not saying a word. Rod was new to the community as well as the church. The reason for decline seemed obvious to him: the congregation was getting older, while at the same time they were so stuck in their ways that they were failing to reach younger people or new people. Rod made what he thought was a positive suggestion. He had read in one of the church's papers that consultants were available to help churches. "Why not ask a consultant to come to our church," Rod said, "to give us some suggestions and ways we might grow?" Some on the board were not sure this was a good idea, while others thought this was a great idea. Anyone who has ever served on a committee knows that when someone has an idea he or she is more than likely put in charge. Rod was instructed to make the necessary contacts.

Two months later, following worship, the church board and a few other interested persons met with the consultant in the church's fellowship hall. The consultant listened to their concerns and even their complaints. He suggested that they have an "Invite A Friend" emphasis at their church. Several churches, he explained, had great success with this program. He suggested that they have invitations printed and then have people from the church personally hand them out to people they know who are not involved in any church. Then on "Invite A Friend Sunday" people in the church make a special effort to welcome them. Following worship the guests are invited to a meal in the fellowship hall. "Spare no expense," the consultant told them. "Explain that the meal is in their honor." There were some good follow-up questions the consultant answered before he left.

Rod thought this was just the thing to do. He was excited about the possibilities. Before people left church that day he told them he knew someone who would probably print the invitations at cost.

George had some words for his pastor as he left church that day. George did not like the idea one bit. "All the young people want to do is have a party," he said. "Church is supposed to be serious. We will never have a party in my church." At the next church meeting George spoke against the plan and had recruited enough people to agree with him that the motion was soundly defeated. Rod was clearly disappointed. Nothing would be done, and attendance in that church would continue to decline.

Proper 24
Matthew 22:15-22

The Word From God

Then the Pharisees went and plotted to entrap him in what he said. (v. 15)

The initial impression persons have when meeting Kurt for the first time is of his positive outlook on life. Kurt works for a national firm as a delivery person, covering the same territory five days a week. Kurt always takes a couple of minutes to speak with his customers as he drops off packages. It's obvious that he enjoys his job and speaking with people. If you were to stand near his truck on most days, you would hear Christian teachings coming from a tape. "Today the lesson was on ..." he says to anyone who asks and then gives a brief summary of what he has heard.

Kurt is not timid when it comes to his faith. "I would probably get fired if my boss knew what I talk about," he admitted one day. One of his stops is a church where he would engage the pastor in some deep theological issues on a regular basis. There were times when the two of them could be seen out in the parking lot debating various issues. The church has always played an important role in Kurt's life. At one point he had aspirations of becoming a pastor and enrolled in a Bible college. Something happened that discouraged him. That seems to be the only subject he is not willing to talk about as he makes his deliveries. He doesn't have to; the hurt is obvious.

One day, quite unexpectedly, Kurt told his friend, "If I had a problem I could never go back to the church I grew up in." By the look on his face he surprised himself with that statement. He went on to explain that if he were experiencing some difficulty in his personal life the people he has known since he was a child would look down on him. "They might even be shocked," he said, speaking of his personal struggles. "They would be quick to point fingers at me." They would tell him he shouldn't think that way and dismiss him as less than a true Christian. He knew the people at his home church all too well.

Fortunately Kurt found a church where people can share openly their struggles and concerns. The openness and caring attitude is what attracted them to that congregation. Kurt says his parents do not understand and would not approve of this church. People in the church where he grew up, he says, could not even imagine a church like the one he now attends.

The difference is, he explained, "If I took a problem to them they would support me 100 percent! They would place their hands on me and pray for me. They would pray that whatever had its grips on me would be released," he says with assurance. They would surround him and show their love and support. "Without a doubt they would be there for me," he says, "no matter what!" With that Kurt was off for another delivery.

Have we in the church become like the Pharisees who stand ready to entrap and accuse?

Proper 25
Deuteronomy 34:1-12

Broken Promises

"I have let you see it with your eyes, but you shall not cross over there." (v. 4b)

Frank was fortunate. Upon graduation from high school he was offered a job at the local tile plant. "I have it made now," Frank told his friends. The tile plant had been a mainstay in that community since the beginning of the century. People who were fortunate enough to be hired there would more than likely retire from that company. There was an unwritten rule: this company treated its employees well, and the employees in turn responded by working 40 or 45 years. Frank worked hard, receiving promotions and pay raises over the years.

Life was great for Frank. Several years after he landed his dream job he married Sarah and was able to buy a modest-sized house in a nice neighborhood with plenty of shade trees. "This will be a wonderful place to raise a family," Frank told Sarah after they moved in. Yes, Frank was the lucky one. He had a job he liked and a nice house, and they would soon have children.

As the years passed Frank continued to work hard. They were able to put money aside for their children's education fund. Both Frank and Sarah wanted to give their children something that was not readily available to them, further education. Later Frank would proudly say that they put all three of their children through college. Their children would be the first to have a college education in their extended families. They were proud of this accomplishment.

Life was just getting better and better for Frank until one day the unthinkable happened. Frank received notice that he would lose his job, effective in only six weeks. Frank stood there feeling numb. He could not believe it. He had worked for this company for over thirty years. This was the only place he had ever worked.

The plant was acquired by a competitor firm that would be closing the plant, the notice read.

Sarah knew something was wrong the moment she saw Frank. That evening, for the first time in his life, Frank sat in his chair and cried. What would he do? He was only 51 years old. He was filled with many questions; where would he get a job at his age? Who would hire him? "My life might as well be over," he told Sarah in a moment of self-defeat. It just was not right. He had worked so hard.

After the initial shock had worn off Frank decided he would do the things he had always wanted to do but never had the time. He became involved in his community. A couple of afternoons each week he volunteered at the library, helping adults learn to read. On other days he would read stories to the children.

During this time he also became more active in his church. He wanted to make a difference in his church, that was what he told the pastor. He began visiting persons during the week, which he really enjoyed.

He made the most of his time, unlike many of his disgruntled friends. When his unemployment ran out he was able to find another job, thanks to the contacts he had made while volunteering. Although he did not earn as much money as he did at his former job he was happy. "This is what God wants me to do," he stated.

Proper 26
Matthew 23:1-12

Julie's Love Shines Through

"All who exalt themselves will be humbled, and all who humble themselves will be exalted." (v. 12)

One warm evening, within sight of her house, Julie found herself in a difficult position, a completely unexpected position, looking down the barrel of a loaded handgun. While this might be a common occurrence in many cities in the United States, it wasn't something that happened in a small, quiet, quaint town nestled between two mountains that does not even have a police force.

In that instant Julie was scared. "I did not know what to do," she said. "I thought he was going to shoot me!" There was no escape either. There was nowhere for her to hide. Julie did the only thing she could think of at that moment. She began talking with the young man who was pointing the gun at her. Julie had taught Sunday School for nearly fifty years and had volunteered at the local school. She knew how to deal with young people. She had dealt with troubled young people before in various situations but nothing like what was unfolding right before her eyes. Julie does not remember what exactly she said. What she does remember is that just as fast as this young man pulled the gun on her he put it back in his belt and began apologizing to her. They talked for twenty minutes or so before he calmed down enough to drive home.

While she might not have acted scared, Julie was upset by the whole incident. It did not take too long for such news to travel through a small town. Before sunset that evening just about everyone in town knew what had happened. Some sitting on their porches warned anyone who happened by of what happened. "The streets are no longer safe," they cried. Others were busy on the telephone, embellishing what had taken place that night in their town.

Somehow or another in the course of their conversation the young man had given Julie his name and address. She wrote him a letter to tell him how much he had frightened her. In the letter she also told him she forgave him for what he had done just as God forgives everyone.

Julie received a letter from this troubled young man the next week. He apologized again, saying he was sorry for what he had put her through. He didn't mean to hurt her or anyone. He was just so mad and so hurt that night. He went on to describe the hurts in his young life. That night when he pulled the gun on Julie he had had a terrible fight with his girlfriend. She told him she no longer wanted to go out with him. His parents were not home at the time. He grabbed the gun from his father's closet and ran out of the house. He was at wits' end. He did not know what to do or where he should go. He just started driving and ended up by Julie's home. He did not know why he stopped in front of her house. He thanked her for listening to him that night and for writing to him.

Julie wrote back, telling him about Jesus. "Jesus can make every wrong right," she wrote. Julie hates to think what might have happened had she not been willing to reach out to this troubled young man.

Proper 27
Matthew 25:1-13

Angie's Grand Adventure

Later the other bridesmaids came also, saying, "Lord, Lord, open to us." But he replied, "Truly I tell you, I do not know you." (vv. 11-12)

Eight-year-old Angie and her family were visiting friends in suburban Washington DC. It was the first time Angie had ever been to a large metropolitan city. She was dazzled by all the people, traffic, and large buildings. Once at their friend's house the children decided to ride bicycles, the two visiting children as well as the two who lived there. Angie's mother told them not to go very far, just around the block a couple of times. After several hours of driving in the car, expending some energy would be the best thing for the children.

Sometime later, when the mothers went looking for the children, all the children were back except for Angie. Upon questioning the other children said they did not know what happened to Angie. They thought she was right behind them on her bike. They turned the corner and waited and waited, but she never turned the corner so they returned home.

The panic-stricken adults quickly got into the car and began driving frantically around the block searching for the missing child. When they did not find Angie around the first block, they expanded their search to the next block and then the next. Her mother kept calling her name, hoping deep down she would hear that familiar voice, "Coming, Mom." After their failed search, they returned to the house, hoping by now Angie would be back safe and sound. When she was not, they called 911. As they waited for the police, all sorts of terrible thoughts filled their minds.

After 45 agonizing minutes, a police car arrived with Angie in the back seat, followed by an older model car with two elderly women. In the front yard was a joyful reunion as mother and father hugged their wayward daughter and smothered her with kisses.

When asked what happened, Angie explained that she was not sure how long a "block" was so when she separated from the other children she just kept going straight. After what the police estimated as fifteen blocks, she came to an overpass and then realized that maybe she had gone too far. She stood on the corner crying.

Just then the two women happened past. They saw Angie standing on the corner crying, so they stopped to ask her what was wrong. Between sobs she managed to say she was lost and then began to cry even harder. "Don't worry, little girl," one of the women tried to assure her. "We'll take you home. Where do you live, honey?" the other woman asked. "Pennsylvania," Angie replied. The two elderly women just looked at each other. As the women were talking with her, a police officer spotted them.

This was not the end of the story. By the time the police officer informed everyone what happened, assuring them that Angie was unharmed, one of the elderly women slowly made her way across the lawn. She told the group that her husband had died just two weeks ago. She was sitting home, all alone, feeling sad that afternoon. Her friend called, suggesting that they go for a drive. A drive would do her good, her friend assured her. It would help her take her mind off other things.

The woman told Angie's mother that for the first time since her husband's death she felt better. "It feels good to help someone else," she said. Somehow or other God's hand brought Angie and this woman together that afternoon.

Proper 28
Matthew 25:14-30

Because We Care

"... to one he gave five talents, to another two, to another one, to each according to his ability." (v. 15)

The man sat in the waiting room of the doctor's office all by himself. He was the last patient of the day. He looked sad, so sad that he caught the attention of the office administrator, Ellen. She decided that since it was the end of the day she would go talk to him to make sure he was all right.

Ellen sat down near him, not identifying herself as an employee. She asked him how he was doing, "I'm doing better than before," he slowly and deliberately said. "Better than before?" Ellen questioned. "Yes," he responded, not looking up to see who was speaking with him. The man told how he and his family had moved from the west coast to the east and were experiencing difficulties. A friend told him there was plenty of work in the east, so they packed everything they could fit into their old station wagon and moved. This was the biggest mistake he made, he told her in no uncertain terms.

The children were having a hard time adjusting to a new school and making new friends. He admitted that he and his wife also were having a hard time getting situated in a new community. He wasn't able to find work either. His only option was working a couple of part-time jobs, barely making enough to feed his family. He told her they were living in shack on the edge of town without any running water. The children complained of being hungry when they went to bed, which made him feel worse. He wanted to be a good father. He had reached the point where he just could not continue like this any longer.

His solution, the only solution he could think of, was to kill his wife and children and then turn the gun on himself, committing suicide. Ellen sat there in shock as this mysterious man continued his story. He had all the plans worked out in his mind, of how and where he was going to do it. He even had a gun. Then one day he received a postcard in the mail from the doctor's office reminding him that his children needed their shots. On the front of the postcard were the words *"Because We Care."* That postcard changed his outlook on life. He thought no one would miss him and his family. He thought no one cared whether they lived or died. He told his wife, "You know the doctor will know if our children do not get their shots." She agreed. For the first time in a very long time he could see his way out of their dilemma. An appointment was made for the children.

Ellen was the person who ordered those postcards. She never gave it a thought as she placed her order. Ellen was unprepared for what this stranger told her. She tried to find the right words, something to make him feel better, but found it difficult. She told him she was glad he did not kill himself and his family. Before she left the office she called several places she knew that would provide assistance for this family, to offer both physical support and emotional support.

Ellen would later tell a friend that she never came any closer to death than she did that afternoon.

Christ The King
Matthew 25:31-46

Take Me Out To The Ball Game!

"Lord, when was it that we saw you hungry or thirsty or a stranger or naked or sick or in prison, and did not take care of you?" (v. 44)

Whenever visiting the community park he could not help but notice ten-year-old Tony and his younger brother. It did not matter what time of day persons went to the park, Tony and his brother were there from early morning until the park closed. At first people would think nothing of seeing them alone. After all, it was summer and lots of kids spend their days at the park. No one knew Tony's brother's name, he was always in the shadow of his bigger, more boisterous brother. At twilight most of the kids would go home. Sometimes a parent or older brother or sister would have to call them. No one ever came looking for Tony and his brother. No one ever saw them with a parent or responsible adult either. They were always by themselves.

Little League baseball was played at the park almost every night during the summer months. Tony and his brother would sit in the bleachers. They would sit in the exact same spot day after day, night after night. What drew attention to Tony was his loud singing. "Take me out to the ball game," Tony and his little brother would sing. "I don't care if I ever get back to the old ball game." At first several parents were annoyed at Tony's disruptive behavior, but as the days turned into weeks, which turned out to be all summer, they would expect to see these two boys. At some point during the game Tony would stand up and start singing. They sat through every game, often leading in cheers for players and teams even though they did not know a single player.

The week school started the best teams were completing in play-off games. Tony and his brother were still at the park as they had been all summer. No one seemed to know anything about these boys. It was as if they were a permanent fixture at that park. It was then that some of the parents became concerned, wondering if they had a home or went to school. Concerned parents would talk with each other during the games, wondering what if anything they should do. Someone suggested calling the police, someone else thought children and youth services should be called. Someone even suggested following the boys "home" to see where they lived. The truth is that no one did anything as summer quickly faded to fall and many other activities.

It's late November now. The days are cooler and shorter. Little League baseball games have long since stopped. The park is deserted most of the time, except for an occasional jogger or someone walking a dog on the weekend. The people who visited the park all summer long are busy doing other things. They forgot all about Tony and his little brother.

Did anyone know what happened to these boys? Did anyone care? What makes this sad is that park is within a stone's throw of three churches. The saddest thing is that it seemed those churches had no intention of reaching out to people like Tony and his brother. They had probably never even noticed the boys.